Great Themes of the Bible

Volume 2

Sarah S. Henrich

Westminster John Knox Press
LOUISVILLE • LONDON

Scripture quotations from the New Revised Standard Version of the Bible are copyright © 1989 by the Division of Christian Education of the National Council of the Churches of Christ in the U.S.A. and are used by permission.

Book design by Sharon Adams

Cover design by Eric Walljasper, Minneapolis, MN
Cover art: Reni, Guido (1575–1642). Moses with the Tablets of the Law. *Galleria Borghese, Rome, Italy.*
Photo Credit: Scala/Art Resource, NY

First edition
Published by Westminster John Knox Press
Louisville, Kentucky

This book is printed on acid-free paper that meets the American National Standards Institute Z39.48 standard. ∞

PRINTED IN THE UNITED STATES OF AMERICA

07 08 09 10 11 12 13 14 15 16 — 10 9 8 7 6 5 4 3 2 1

Library of Congress Cataloging-in-Publication Data is on file at the Library of Congress, Washington, D.C.

ISBN-13: 978-0-664-23064-7
ISBN-10: 0-664-23064-4

Great Themes of the Bible

Also available from Westminster John Knox Press

Great Themes of the Bible, Volume 1 by W. Eugene March

Contents

Preface

The Bible is a rich and varied collection of writings developed over thousands of years. Those who wrote the Bible were people who celebrated, lamented, worshiped, and tried to make some sense of life in reference to God. These people lived in diverse cultures and spoke a variety of languages seldom learned in our time. They have left us a legacy whose meaning continues to be debated. The very intensity of debate points to our continued passionate engagement with the God of these writings.

This volume has been created to explore biblical writings by using various themes as "probes" to get below the surface, make connections, and notice nuances of meaning. It is not designed to immerse readers in the scholarly debates that abound in regard to almost every biblical phrase. Decisions about some of those debates do shape the volume, but detailed analysis of them would not be possible or even useful in these thematic probes.

It has been my particular pleasure to work in both Old and New Testament because New Testament theologians, from Mary to Jesus to Paul to the disciples to members of the early communities we call Christian, claimed the Old Testament as their Scripture. It is from the Old Testament as Scripture that they sought God more deeply, not least in the person of Jesus of Nazareth. This book offers a wonderful opportunity to dig more deeply into the long history of God's interactions with humankind and to see God's steadfast purpose for the thriving of creation.

I hope that this volume provides a jumping-off point for Bible study as a lifelong process. I hope even more that it helps readers catch a glimpse, at least, of God's faithfulness as grounds for human hope and commitment to a flourishing creation.

I must offer thanks to friends and colleagues who have continued to expand my understanding of the Old Testament; to Luther Seminary, which provided sabbatical time enabling me to do this work; and to Donald K. McKim for his calm support through the process.

Chapter One

Death

When you take away their breath, they die and return
to their dust.

Ps. 104:29

None of us really "gets" death. We know persons who have
died. Perhaps we have been with or seen them at the time of
death. In death we come face to face with the greatest mystery:
what once was is no longer. Did a living being, a tapestry of memories, expectations, responses, emotions, simply cease to be? Our
minds and hearts wrestle with the utter strangeness of death.
There must be something more, we think, some life after this one.
Humans experience light, sounds, visitations, and encounters
with those who have died. If we are waiting with longing for justice, if we have seen lives end in an untimely way, we wonder why
a just God would deprive people of God's own gift of life.

We imagine some sort of life in death and have many ways to
express our hopes of life beyond biological death. People "pass on,"
"pass over," "pass away," "go home" to realms beyond our own. We
also use "death" to describe persons and places who seem not fully
alive in their earthly existence. Think of "dead to the world" as a
description of sleep; the deadening of pain; a room is "dead" when
sounds do not resonate; a nonresponsive audience may be "dead."

In this patchwork of ways in which we think of and imagine

1

death we follow those who went before us. In the Bible, there are as many different ways of considering and talking about death as there are among us. Two differences between contemporary folks and our biblical ancestors, however, should be noted. First, our ancestors were more intimately acquainted with death. People died younger and more publicly than we are accustomed to. Wars, plagues, lack of sanitation, the dangers of childbirth, and diseases were constant companions. Second, our ancestors believed more easily than we in transcendent realms and their invisible but quite real inhabitants. Their questions about death generated an even wider array of responses than among us. We find many of these responses in the Bible.

Old Testament

In the Old Testament we will be working with English translations of quite a few terms that describe death, dying, perishing, and even sleep as death (Deut. 31:16). Sometimes these terms refer to biological death. At others they seem metaphorical for a state akin to biological death but not identical with it. In addition, biological death itself was weighed differently in Israel over the centuries of the Old Testament's writings. Although death could be seen and accepted as a natural (albeit often quite sad) part of God's order, it was also sometimes identified as a consequence of sin, a punishment for sin, or simply the work of a power contrary to God. Death might come through old age, battle, trickery, punishment, illness, hunger, or murder. The dead generally were dead or "sleeping"; no immortal soul lived on, returned to God, or reunited with another body. The dead do live in their ongoing descendents and the legacy of their lives.

Biological Death

Human beings died natural deaths, often at great ages, in the Old Testament. The stories of Genesis provide a good starting place. First Sarah, then Abraham died in Canaan (Gen. 23:1–25:8), both very old and much blessed. For both, as for their descendents in

Genesis, death is not represented as enemy. Long life is a gift of God, but death is not the withdrawing of the gift or an expression of God's anger. Abraham is said to have been "gathered to his people" after burial, an unusual phrase applied also only to Jacob and Isaac (Gen. 35:29; 49:33). If it is a reference to an afterlife, it is certainly an oblique one that gives no information.

These deaths are related along with genealogical information suggesting that dead persons lived on to some degree through the life of the family. This sensibility gives added pathos to Jacob's reluctance to send Benjamin, the only surviving son of his beloved Rachel, into Egypt (Gen. 42:38; 44:20). Were Benjamin to die, Jacob believed his last living link to Rachel would have died with him. Psalm 128 summarizes the happiness that is available to "everyone who fears the LORD." It bespeaks a modest, domestic peaceable kingdom with everything working as it should. When things did not go so well, when untimely death made impossible fertility, family, or peace, more explanation was needed.

Death is initially associated with the departure of Adam and Eve from Eden. The harmony of a domestic and agricultural life was interrupted by their attempt to deceive God. Deceit disrupted their existence and brought death in many forms. Adam and Eve would die at much younger ages. They were exposed to the dangers of a world with poisonous snakes (animals had become dangerous to humans) and to bodies where much could go wrong (as in childbirth). More importantly, inexplicable motives drew human beings to kill one another, as in the story of Cain and Abel. Death had great power to destroy all that one might hope for in life. When death did not come at the end of a long and fruitful life, it could be a punishment from God; the work of some malevolent power, superior to humans but inferior to God; the result of chance; or the consequences of misbehavior. In such cases God might be called upon to restore the dead to life, as we shall see.

Death Wielded by Harsh Powers

In one apocryphal story (Tob. 6:10–18) a demon had killed off seven husbands of a young woman on their wedding nights. Their deaths were not attributed to misbehavior or wickedness on the part of the bridegrooms. Rather, they were victims of a demon whose criteria for killing, whatever it may have been, did not operate by God's code. Demons or other invisible powers could and did bring about death. Because of their power, the righteous as well as the unrighteous might be felled by death.

The most important struggle over undeserved death in the Old Testament takes place in the book of Job. Through a malevolent power (Job 1:6–12) Job, a profoundly devout man, loses to death his family, his livestock, and very nearly himself. Weak, ill, and bereft of all the joys of his righteous life, Job knows and will not be persuaded otherwise that the calamities which have beset him are not because of his failings. He had been and should have continued to be the contented family man from Psalm 128. Yet, assailed by the power of Satan, Job's life becomes such a misery that he wants to die just to be free of God's eye and power. Job could barely stand to live in a world of injustice where the good and the innocent are slain at whim. Where is God in such a world? (Job 3:3). Convinced that death would take him to a place where God would no longer see or "target" him, Job wished for death as a kind of substitute peace for the peaceful life he had lost. In 7:20–21, he challenges God to tell him what unpardonable sins he has committed that have resulted in his cruel punishment. Job is mistaken (somewhat) in attributing his misery to God. But it is telling that Job cannot believe that the God he knew and worshiped would be so unjust, so unfaithful, so egregiously cruel. Job himself experiences a kind of death of his confidence, hope, and trust in God. He might as well be biologically dead (see also 9:22–24).

Job's complaint is never really answered, but he does not die. God speaks to him finally, challenging him with the question, "Have the gates of death been revealed to you, or have you seen the gates of deep darkness?" (Job 38:17). A human being is not able to understand the ways of God. Where cause and effect seem clear to us and important in creating a reliable universe, God cannot be reliably predicted in the creating of life or death. Job is chastened for imagining that he knows enough to understand the mysteries of God even though God's own self-description and covenants ought to be the source of Job's hope for a reliable universe.

Death as Part of the "Scheme of Things"

The difficulty of coming to grips with death and "understanding" it, whether as reward, punishment, or random event, is at the fore in two other Wisdom books. In Proverbs, the way of the loose woman, or foolishness—that is, straying from the path commanded by God—leads to death (Prov. 2:18; 5:5; 7:27). All who hate wisdom "love death" (8:36). All who love wisdom find that righteousness "delivers from death" (11:4; 12:28; 13:14). Did Job believe that the teaching of the wise is a "fountain of life" enabling one to "avoid the snares of death"? No wonder he was so angry, so betrayed, so desirous of death. For Job, real foolishness had been to trust in these words. Yet Proverbs holds to this message. For its writer, truth is told here—death is held at bay by wisdom and righteousness. Perhaps he means that one's reputation will ensure that one is remembered and "lives" on in that way. He does not say. The two views of death are side by side in Scripture.

Meanwhile, Ecclesiastes (also called Qoheleth) disagrees with Proverbs. The writer has two premises: (1) human beings cannot know their end, when or how it will come; and (2) God's ways are inscrutable. Ecclesiastes therefore enjoins a modest life on God's followers. They are to eat, drink, and enjoy their work, in other words, enjoy God's creation, and not strive for glory. The writer's position does not spring from naiveté. His words could be those of the bitterly experienced Job: "And I thought the dead, who have already died, more fortunate than the living, who are still alive; but better than both is the one who has not yet been, and has not seen the evil deeds that are done under the sun" (Eccl. 4:2–3). He observes that one has no more power over the day of death than over the wind (Eccl. 8:8), suggesting that walking in the ways of righteousness may not matter as much as Proverbs proclaims. "The same fate," he says, "comes to all, to the righteous and the wicked, to the good and the evil, to the clean and the unclean. . . . The same fate comes to everyone" (9:2–3). Nonetheless, life is good and death is not. Death is the end of everything; there is no reward. (On the emptiness of Sheol, see 9:10.) Yet death is not in and of itself evil. When one dies, "the dust returns to the earth as it was, and the breath returns to God who gave it" (12:7). This writer does not imagine that God uses death as punishment or test. It is just the end.

Death as Punishment

Because God has the power to create and destroy, the relationship of death and deity is an intricate one. God has provided a world and the gift of life to be enjoyed as long as possible, yet to punish or test would be to deprive humans of that which they most value—life.

In the story of Tamar and Judah (Gen. 38) we can see how God's disapproval is educed as a cause of death. Judah's sons marry Tamar and die before having any children with her. God is said to have put the first two to death for wickedness (including the wickedness of Onan, who would not beget children that "would not be his"). Judah must give Tamar to his last son as wife in order to have children to carry on his brother's name. Judah delays out of fear that he too will die. Here there is fear that God may be punishing. Death is unnatural, early, and seemingly—although not actually—unwarranted. The story moves on from this premise, as Tamar cleverly cares for her own future by conceiving a child to continue the family name. Not only do we see that God punishes those who do not keep the law, but we also see the importance of descendents as a way to continue the life of one who has died. We will come back to this principle later.

God also used death as a weapon in the struggle to free Israel from Egypt. Warnings and choices of life or death faced Pharaoh and his people (note that in Exod. 9:20 even Pharaoh's officers fear God and behave differently from their king). Defiance of God, who was working on behalf of his enslaved people, brought death. Death as penalty for defiance can also be found in the codes of Israel. Exodus 19, 21, and 31 explain that death will be meted out to those who transgress the boundaries of God's holiness (the holy mountain, the Sabbath) or who bring about the death of other humans. The Levitical code lists which transgressions should result in death. People could know the code and make their choices, even as Pharaoh had done. In all these situations, death came upon those who willfully and knowingly defied God's command in such a way that God and/or God's people in community were in some way diminished or harmed. Destructive injustice could merit the punishment of death—the cessation of human power and relationship. Death might also be a consequence of such behavior rather than a punishment for it.

Typical of the kind of destruction that occasioned death for the perpetrators would be human sacrifice. In Leviticus 20:2–5, God inveighs against the sacrifice of children to Molech. Such sacrifice would both blaspheme God's name and also kill a human being, a part of God's covenant people—both taboo behaviors. In the same way, those who claimed to be mediums or wizards, using the dead to seek knowledge of or manipulate events, could not continue to live. God or God's chosen prophet were to be the only reliable sources of information.

In the terrible episode where Saul defies God's law against the use of wizards and mediums to conjure the dead, Saul forces the medium of Endor to bring up the dead Samuel (1 Sam. 28). Saul broke his own (and God's) laws in his desperate attempt to learn the future to control it. As a result of this deed, Saul himself became as one almost dead; he also received news of death and destruction. Notice that Samuel's shade (ghost) is somehow able to be conjured from the realms of the dead, suggesting that some form of shadowy other-life was imagined by some in Israel. That which arises from the ground is described as a "divine being," which may have to do with its being other than mortal. Samuel is angered that he has been disturbed. The disturbance reminds us that the dead were often understood to be "sleeping" (see also Job 14:12; Pss. 13:3; 22:29, for example).

If a life was destructive to community well-being, God might elect to remedy that situation with death. Consider the deaths of

Goliath, seemingly invincible champion of the Philistines (1 Sam. 17), and of Nabal (1 Sam. 25), whose inhospitable and foolish behavior almost cost the lives of all his young men and therefore his whole extended household. These are but two examples of how the larger community is protected by the death of one person.

God Restores Life from Death
Psalm 104 elegantly pictures God's will for life and God's power to sustain it. Life is God's good gift (Ps. 104:30), and death is simply its cessation (Ps. 104:29). When the wicked and all others die, they are "consumed from the earth" and are "no more." The love of God that "rules over all" (Ps. 103:19) has created intricate order with death as a part. When death occurs out of the "natural order" and is seriously destructive of community, God may elect to forestall or remedy death. The prophets Elijah and Elisha both raise young men from death when challenged by grieving mothers (one widowed and one with an old husband) for whom sons establish them in the community (1 Kgs. 17:8–24; 2 Kgs. 4:32–37). When the widow's (woman not of Israel) son is restored to life, she confesses that Elijah is truly "a man of God, and that the word of the LORD in your mouth is truth." God's power over life and breath (1 Kgs. 17:21) is clear. Just the bones of the prophet Elisha were able to bring a man back to life (2 Kgs. 13:20–21).

Two exceptions to the power of death appear in the Old Testament: Elijah ascends to heaven in a chariot of fire (2 Kgs. 2:11), and Enoch (Gen. 5:24) simply is taken to walk with God. These two who did not die but lived somehow in heavenly realms became important in the history of Jews and Christians as figures able to mediate knowledge. Either may return to earth to announce the coming of the end times.

New Testament

In the New Testament, as in the Old, only God is immortal (1 Tim. 6:16). Everyone else, including Jesus, is subject to death, although Elijah and Enoch seem to be important exceptions to that rule. (Hebrews 11:5 mentions Enoch. The possibility of Elijah's return creates high expectation about John the Baptist and at the time of Jesus' crucifixion.) At the same time, the New Testament emerged from the high energy of change, expectation, and experience of the presence of God's Holy Spirit that followed the crucifixion and resurrection of Jesus of Nazareth. The whole New Testament is shaped by the conviction that God has changed the relationship of humans to death by the resurrection of Jesus. The New Testament contends that Jesus is the one in whom all must believe if they are to experience resurrection into joy. Such a claim posits that all humans will truly die. It also alludes to the possibility of a miserable life after death.

The New Testament also uses the language of being "dead" in life. Death is a way of describing distance from God or rejection of God's saving grace (often in the form of rejecting Jesus as God's saving Messiah). Luke's parable of the father with two sons in 15:11–32 speaks of a brother having been "dead" and his coming back to the family as a return to "life." Here biological life and death are not indicated but rather separation—created by the son's rejection—from one's people, one's father, the source of one's identity. John's Gospel also insists that those who believe in Jesus have eternal life in the midst of biological life; those who do not believe are in death in the midst of life. Life and death are metaphors for being connected to God or not, to Jesus, to one's community. The metaphors have power precisely because of the unbridgeable distinction between life and death and our inherent preference for life.

Is Death Real for Christians?

Different ways of describing what happens in death and after it sit side by side in the New Testament. Does one die, as Paul wishes to do, and find oneself "with Christ" (Phil. 1:21–23)? Does one simply "sleep" until that final day comes in which one will be with Christ (1 Thess. 4:13; John 11:11)? In a way, it does not matter. Who really knows and can say what is on the other side of the cessation of breath? Paul most fully and beautifully affirms the truth that gives the New Testament its reason for being: ~~nothing~~, not ~~even death (or life for that matter) will be able to separate us from the love of God~~ in Christ Jesus (~~Rom. 8:38–39~~). Death is real biologically, but it has no final or spiritual power. Real life, the life lived for God, is or will be shared by those who inherit the kingdom through Jesus. Paul is clear that there will be judgment, for which he prays that believers be prepared. But for the righteous, life will be eternal.

Paul, unlike John, does not claim that believers already have eternal life, but that they will be raised to it. Matthew and Luke speak the same way. The power of God demonstrated by Elijah and Elisha is the same power God wields to overcome first Jesus' death and later the deaths of his followers. In Acts 2:24 Peter says, "But God raised him up, having freed him from death, because it was impossible for him to be held in its power." The Creator and Lord of life will sustain the lives of his people baptized into his raised-up Son. Death is a lesser power, no longer to be feared.

Jesus' power to restore to life is evidence of this powerful will of God for life. The same power is wielded by his disciples in Acts, where Peter raises Tabitha from death (Acts 9:40–43), where Paul raises Eutyches (Acts 20:9–10) and even thwarts his own death (Acts 28:3–5). It is healing power super-sized. Being healed or raised does not mean that those who love God will not again grow ill and die. Avoiding biological death is always temporary. Stephen, the first martyr, raises his eyes to heaven and sees the risen Jesus as Son of Man at God's right hand as he dies (Acts 7:56–60). This vision is held out to all believers, a vision that inspires the confidence that death will not have the last word.

Reflections

In the Bible human beings die for various reasons. Whether death is the "wages of sin" or whether it is part of a natural process is not clear. On matters of death, human beings who are subject to it cannot see into its processes and causes. On matters of death, however, human beings dare trust that God is stronger than death. There are numerous instances where death is reversed or prevented throughout both Testaments. There is a spectrum of beliefs about death from permanency to impermanency. One might continue to live only through honorable memories and descendents or through the restoration of a people.

At the other end of the spectrum is the conviction of bodily resurrection. The New Testament witnesses that for those who are alive to God in Jesus Christ, death has been destroyed. We still experience biological death, however. But that such a death would be the end of our relationship with God is denied. Jesus' resurrection makes a new life, a new creation available universally, although not all will be raised to joy. New life comes in glimpses now, but its full reality awaits either individual death or the "end of days" when God restores all creation.

Questions for Discussion

1. What do you think happens when we die? Does it matter to you? Why or why not?
2. Confident that death is not ultimate, as Luke would say, "How then shall we live?"
3. How and why is it—or is it not—appropriate for Christians to grieve the deaths of their loved ones? What about the catastrophic deaths of others in a natural disaster or a war?
4. What difference does the Holocaust (and subsequent events of genocide, as in Rwanda or the former Yugoslavia) make in your thinking about God as Lord of life and death?

Chapter Two

Discipleship

For we are God's servants, working together.
1 Cor. 3:9

By definition a disciple is a learner. The word "disciple" comes from Latin and simply means learner or student. Our consideration of the theme discipleship must include attention to themes of learning, teaching, and following, all different word families in Hebrew and Greek just as they are in English. In the Bible there is also a way of speaking of discipleship that is quite unfamiliar to contemporary folks—that of sonship. To be described as the "son" of or "child" of someone can refer to biological connections, but it may also refer to being a follower, a person who in some way resembles a teacher or leader (e.g., sons of the prophets). We must, therefore, also look carefully at the vocabulary of being a child as a biblical way of talking about discipleship. Each of these different word families in English carries different weight and nuance.

Disciples as learners do not always understand their teacher or live in accord with what they have learned. In the history of human beings in relation to God, the teaching of God mediated through dreams, visions, Scripture, a prophet, Jesus, or Christian believers like Paul or John has been interpreted, received, and taken to heart in many and often competing variations. The Bible is astonishingly honest at showing us many different and lively ways of being disciples of God.

Old Testament

Israel: A Community of Disciples

Central to Jewish Scripture and identity is the proclamation of Deuteronomy 6:4–5, "Hear, O Israel: The LORD is our God, the LORD alone. You shall love the LORD your God with all your heart, and with all your soul, and with all your might." This straightforward description of Israel's relationship with God and the call to live in such a relationship of love is the heart of faith and life. It is so important that both preceding and subsequent verses frame it with commands to "teach" these words to every generation (6:1, 6–9). In Deuteronomy 11:19 we hear, "Teach them to your children, talking about them when you are at home and when you are away, when you lie down and when you rise." It is teaching God's words, making them visible, and having them in mind always, that keeps relationship with God alive for humans. If discipleship means being in a position of learning from one's teacher or guide, Jewish life revolves around discipleship.

Moses himself was taught by God (Exod. 4:12, 15) in order to teach others (Exod. 13:9; Deut. 4:1, 5, 14) that they might then teach their children forever. The teaching of God's word, will, and ways shaped the call of Moses and the prophets, of judges and kings. Indeed, it shaped the life of Israel. Because of the centrality of learning about God in order to follow God (and vice versa), all of Israel was called to be teachers, learners, followers, disciples. The whole people of Israel was expected to strive to be disciples of God, although the word "disciple" is not used in the Old Testament. It does not have to be. The "disciples" are the people of Israel, however well and badly they fulfill their calling. Discipleship is about continuing to live according to God's call and covenant. Discipleship is a way of life for God's children in covenant relationship. Yet there is nothing simple about such a life. How might one best follow God? It is not hard to see why teachers and teaching were of central importance for a people all of whom were expected to be learners or disciples the better to serve God.

God: Israel's Teacher and Disciple Maker

Often in Scripture we find prayers for God's continued presence and teaching of the people. In 1 Kings 8:36, King Solomon prays at the first assembly in the new temple, asking God to hear in heaven, even when the people sin, and then to "forgive the sin of your servants, your people Israel, when you teach them the good way in which they should walk." Throughout the Psalms Israel prays in gratitude for teaching and hope of continued instruction. We can read this in contemporary terms as gratitude and hope for God's continued activity of "discipling." Psalm 25 has numerous references to the Lord as teacher. God is not a teacher of abstract theological doctrine, but the one who teaches "your paths" as well as "your truth" (Ps. 25:4–5). Nor is God a teacher only of elite students or those who have leisure and mental endowment for learning. The Lord is praised for being the one to teach "the humble his way" and to "instruct sinners" (Ps. 25:8–9). Teaching the next generation is a way to make true disciples or learners of them. A clear description of this process as a reflection on God's historic call appears in Psalm 78:5–7. It is easy to see in these verses the many ways in which being a disciple is described. Children are to be taught that they might "know," "rise up and tell," "set their hope in God," "not forget," "keep," be "faithful," not be "stubborn and rebellious." In these ways and many others the proper behavior of God's disciples, the people of Israel, is set out. Psalm 78 sets out a way of life as a follower of God that would be right at home in the New Testament as well.

Other Teachers in Israel

In addition to the position of discipleship in which all of Israel found itself, there were also within Israel certain teachers or interpreters with smaller groups of followers. Also, some particular activities within Israel's social and religious culture may have demanded particular training of individuals or groups. In such cases "followers" or "learners" might refer more narrowly to a smaller group within Israel. There are hints in Scripture of the existence of this understanding of discipleship, an understanding that precedes and clarifies some of the New Testament emphases. For instance, in 1 Chronicles 25:8 in the Greek Old Testament, there is a passing reference to teacher and pupils, taking for granted that these categories existed among God's musicians and prophets. In this case "mature" one describes the teacher and the young is in parallel to "learners." One could connect oneself to a group for instruction, here in relation to music, and be described as a disciple or learner, the same word being translated in two different ways.

Also interesting is a brief description in 2 Chronicles 17:7–10 where Jehosophat's good beginning as king in Israel is exemplified by his decision to send out persons to teach in the cities of Judah (the southern kingdom after the division of Israel into two parts). The king's officials take the "book of the law of the LORD" and go into all the cities to teach. Presumably the teachers were themselves reliable interpreters of Scripture who had learned to read and understand it. We can see how important the "teaching" of the Lord's will and ways was to Israel's role as a true disciple of God. In Isaiah 8:16 the command comes to the prophet from the Lord to "bind up the testimony, seal the teaching among my disciples." It is clear from the verse itself and from preceding verses in the chapter and the larger book that God makes a distinction between who is and who is not truly a disciple within Israel itself. Disciples are those who hear the teaching and live faithfully in relation to it. Those who are not disciples fail on one or both counts.

The possibility of failure of discipleship is a lively and often realized one in Scripture. Failure of discipleship did not automatically oust folk from God's people. Part of discipleship in the Old Testament is learning how to ask for, receive, and trust in God's forgiveness. Israel was God's. The strength of covenant bonds and lack of choice about being part of the people led to the use of two sets of terms to describe the relationship: those of the household and of king and subject most often describe Israel's relationship to God. Israel is child of God, bride of God, servant or slave of God, a member of the household of which God is head. Also, the language of kings and subjects is used. Neither of these paradigms works nearly as well in the New Testament world, as we shall see.

Lest we forget, that sense of being truly a follower of God by attending to godly wisdom is put forward by the books Wisdom, Proverbs, and Ecclesiastes. Each of these claims to be written by a teacher whose ardent students will find wisdom for life in the writings. Not everyone is imagined as a student, and those who are such students might well be considered disciples. Such disciples are devoted to a way of life, a way of thinking about God as much as to an individual teacher. Teaching the ways of God to those who wish to learn continued to be of great importance during the intertestamental period, not least among Jews who no longer lived in Israel. Such persons, like the New Testament believers after them, had to serve kings who were not anointed by God. Scattered around the Mediterranean, they were distant from the household of Israel. In such circumstances, discipleship requires a more conscious and often countercultural choice. The Wisdom of Ben Sirach, the Wisdom of Solomon, 4 Maccabees, *Letter of Aristeas*, Pseudo-Phocylides, and many more labored to write for students, perhaps even schools (see Sir. 51:23, "house of instruction"). One has only to dip into any of these teaching books to see that it is a way of life that is being promulgated, not simply expertise in some subject area. The seeking of wisdom and the importance of learning have been hallmarks of God's people from the most ancient period through this very day. The rabbinic inheritance wherein students clustered around a rabbi for learning was an important component of handing down God's teaching (in diverse ways) from the first century CE onward; it kept alive Jewish communities around the world and continues to this day.

New Testament

A New Sense of God's People
The collection of books we call the New Testament is, broadly speaking, about two things: it tells us of Jesus of Nazareth,

claimed as Messiah of the God of the Jews by his followers, and it relates how Jesus' followers both understood him and gathered communities around their convictions. Each book of the New Testament shared with its original audience (and shares now with us) the theological understandings of its writer, who was a disciple of the teacher and prophet Jesus. Each book reveals to us the intense sorting out of what beliefs, customs, and practices will define these new communities of God's people "in" Jesus Christ. The New Testament is about discernment of true disciples and discipleship in the midst of the complexities of ancient cultures. The New Testament, unlike the Old, can take little for granted in the shaping of new religious communities. There are no family histories that bind folk together, no geographical center for life or worship, no dominant interpretation of Scripture, not even clarity about what might and what might not be Scripture. Discipleship, therefore, is constitutive of the New Testament in ways quite different from its role in the Old.

By the first century CE the world of both Jews and later Christians had become larger and more complex. Jews lived outside of Jerusalem in communities around the Mediterranean, often by choice. Christianity began its journey in these same communities and quickly spread among persons with no previous ties to Judaism. Both Jews and Christians needed ways to identify believers and to deepen their identity as a people. (On a new identity for Christians, see 1 Pet. 2:10.) During this time "rabbi," once a general title of honor like "sir," became a title for an honored teacher who gathers students about himself. This title is used for Jesus in some New Testament documents.

In the New Testament period, among the expressions of Jewish faith were numerous "schools." We hear of Pharisees, Sadducees, and scribes, for instance. We know of a group of Jews whose devotion to torah led to mass suicide at Masada. We hear of Essenes and, in Philo's writing, Therapeutae. These groups with theological, ethical, and political commitments pepper the pages of the New Testament (and intertestamental Jewish texts) with argument and energy.* It is clear that Jewish belief was far from monolithic. Naturally, early Christians appeared as one group among many gathered around Rabbi Jesus.

Rabbi Jesus

This title shows up more frequently in John's Gospel than elsewhere; it is not used at all by Luke, and Matthew disavows it. In John 1:38 and 49, Jesus is twice called rabbi, once by disciples of John the Baptist and once by Nathaniel, who identifies Jesus also as Son of God and Messiah. (References to the disciples of John, who is also called rabbi, and to those of Jesus appear in John 3:25 and 4:2.) The connection of a rabbi to his disciples is clear. Jesus' own disciples call him rabbi in John 4:31, 9:2, and John 11:8. His devoted disciple Mary Magdalene also so identifies him in 20:16. We can see that Jesus' teaching and healing ministry and his gathering of students, or disciples, made it seem natural to call him rabbi in these early texts. Nicodemus, who had been watching Jesus' work, comes to him and greets him as "rabbi" (John 3:2). Both men are "teachers in Israel" with very different kinds of insights, Jesus' garnered from his relationship with Israel's God. Jesus does not dispute the title in John's Gospel. In Matthew's, however, there is significant controversy about honoring any person as "rabbi" or "father," another honorific term for a leader/teacher. In Matthew 23:7–11, Jesus is an "instructor," God the only teacher and Father, and all followers are "siblings" (not "students" as the NRSV translates it). All these references remind us how important Jesus' teaching role was and how notable in his own time his disciples were. In all four Gospels, they attended not only to the verbal content of Jesus' teaching but tried—not always

---

*A word of caution here: The New Testament by no means presents a historically accurate description of such groups or their adherents. Out to distinguish following Jesus as the proper way to be the people of God, early writers often created a negative portrait of other groups in order to sharpen the contrast. Even so, Luke is considerably less hostile to scribes and Pharisees than Matthew, for example.

successfully—to shape their own lives in accord with it. Even Judas, a disciple whose betrayal is the more grievous because of his having followed Jesus, calls Jesus rabbi (Mark 14:45 and Matt. 26:25, 49).

The fact that Jesus is often said to teach "with authority," unlike the scribes and Pharisees, means that those who found Jesus' teaching authoritative would form groups. They tried to deepen their understanding and lead lives in accord with Jesus' teaching. These folks were the disciples who are so often mentioned but almost never named in the New Testament. The *mathetes* were disciples as learners. They followed Jesus seeking to participate in and understand the kingdom of God that was "at hand." Disciples are not the same as the Twelve or the apostles. Rather, the word describes those who devoted themselves to the teachings and authority of Jesus. In Acts 1:15, for instance, the disciples number about one hundred and twenty, a number which increases both in Jerusalem and around the known world throughout Acts. The word "disciple" often substitutes for "Christian," although Luke (the writer of Acts) does know that both words exist. In Acts 11:26 we are told that "disciples" were first called Christians in Antioch. Whether or not this is historically accurate, it provides us with an understanding of who disciples were as Luke saw it.

Luke's understanding of what was required of disciples is concisely, if somewhat negatively, expressed in Luke 14:26–33. Here the picture of a disciple is one who has renounced primary allegiance to anything or anyone other than Jesus and God whom he brings among us. Nothing can come before that commitment. In Luke 12 a constructive picture emerges as Jesus addresses his disciples with words of wisdom about their lives. Promising that it is their "Father's good pleasure to give [them] the kingdom," Jesus compares discipleship to being a wise and faithful manager. The task for each is comprehensive care of the others in the household. Luke 12, the central and keystone chapter of a twenty-four-chapter Gospel, is all about discipleship. What does it mean to follow Jesus? How difficult is it? How will disciples be cared for in the real world? Jesus offers words of reassurance about a life lived as disciple for those who heard his gospel then and now. The vocation of a faithful and savvy disciple is to create an environment for the thriving of God's creation.

While Luke presents a relatively positive view of the Twelve and other disciples, in Mark's Gospel the picture is darker. All disciples are slow to understand the one whom they follow and the nature of his authority. Even the twelve who journey with Jesus continue to compete for honor and position. (See the account of James and John in Mark 10:35. See also Matthew 20:21–23, where their mother pleads their case.) In spite of receiving special instruction from Jesus on occasion, in spite of being nearby at the time of miraculous healings or feedings, disciples worry about their own welfare, not least in the story of the storm at sea where Jesus questions how much they trust and understand him (Matt. 8:23–27; Mark 4:34–41; Luke 8:22–25).

We get a sense of how difficult it is for persons deeply immersed in their cultures to reshape their lives in accord with faith in this mysterious Jew. Jesus had powers heretofore attributed to God and yet walked among them, a man who became tired, thirsty, hungry. What does a disciple of this Jesus hope for? How does a disciple live? The Twelve miss the gist of true discipleship, which Jesus clarifies as serving others (Matt. 20:25–28; Mark 10:43–45; Luke 22:25–27; John 13:3–17). The most faithful of them wonder at times (Matt. 19:27–30; Mark 10:28–31; Luke 18:28–30). When Jesus died, the disciples likely feared that it had all been a dream. For some, Jesus' resurrection restored their hope and confidence.

In the New Testament, because "disciples" is a bigger category than "the Twelve," we see that disciples include ordinary women and men of Jesus' time and place. This becomes important in Acts. The power of what and how Jesus taught, including also the "teaching" quality of his miracles, which showed God's power at work in the world for good, gathered a crowd of followers. Such followers longed for and received what Jesus had to give: hope that God's power had returned to the world in their behalf; hope that trust in Jesus was truly trust in God; and hope that life in accord with Jesus' teaching (deeply Jewish and scriptural) was somehow new life. They felt their way into this life, stumbling at times, turning fearful and turning tail. But disciples of Jesus celebrated their new communities, shared the message, and sought the transformation wrought by worship of a living God. Jesus was indeed their teacher. The gift of teaching was given also to others after him through the Holy Spirit. The process of discernment of discipleship continues.

Paul and Discipleship

Curiously, outside of the Gospels and Acts, the word "disciple" is not used. Paul is passionately concerned to shape communities of people given new life through Jesus. Perhaps he can dispense with the word "disciple" because his letters are "in-house," written only for gatherings of those who already seek to follow Jesus. It is helpful to remember that Paul's letters were all composed earlier than the Gospels. As Paul builds up these small groups of believers, he uses the language of kinship to break down powerful old family systems and establish new ways of interacting among those who were adopted as children of God. In addition, Paul uses the language of "in Christ" as a way to describe the baptized as a group. Paul certainly writes as if he hopes his hearers will listen to him as their teacher, as do the authors of the other New Testament letters (e.g., John and Peter). They all write so much instruction and encouragement to new ways of life. At the same time Paul seems to eschew any self-understanding as the teacher within a circle of his own disciples (1 Cor. 1:11–17; 3:4–11). He encourages discipleship with Christ.

"Disciple," like "rabbi," is a term that some writers want to avoid, for it suggests a social organization that is not within their theological or cultural understanding. Nonetheless, as in the Old Testament, which does not generally use this term, "disciple" as one who learns and seeks to discern and follow a way of life describes those who form a new and distinctive group "in Christ."

Questions for Discussion

1. Why do you think Jesus' disciples were subject to fears and uncertainties about his role and theirs? What worries you as a follower, however hesitant or strong?
2. Whom do you trust to help you discern the best way(s) to be a disciple? This sort of discernment has long been part of the work of churches. In our own day, guidance abounds in books, blogs, conversations, television programs, and major magazines, not to mention various best-sellers. Where do you seek guidance? What criteria matter to you as you imagine discipleship in the twenty-first century?
3. What do you see as most important in being a disciple? When you hear Jesus' challenges to "take up your cross" or "become servant of all," how is your life impacted? Or, on the other hand, do you picture your discipleship in line with Luke 12:42–43 or Matthew 25:32–46? If so, how?
4. How might the picture of the relationships among disciples in Matthew 18 matter in your group interactions?
5. Since Paul does not use "disciple" as a term and seems to have less interest in Jesus as a teacher, does it seem right to take Romans 12–15 or Galatians 5:22–6:5, for instance, as instructions for disciples?

Chapter Three

Faith

The scripture, foreseeing that God would justify the Gentiles by faith, declared the gospel beforehand to Abraham, saying, "All the Gentiles shall be blessed in you."

Gal. 3:8

Faith is central to the relationship of human beings to God and one another. Faith, in fact, is what makes such relationships possible. At the deepest level, people live by convictions that cannot be proven but can only be experienced and trusted. The faith we live by is a confident trust in the value or truth of another person or idea. Faith might be placed in one's spouse, for instance, or in the scientific method, the value of education, the American way. Whatever the object of faith might be, faith itself is trust. One can, therefore, have faith and lose it, be no longer able to trust. Indeed, part of the very process of growing up is learning to understand and prove resilient when our immature faith fails us.

In the Bible, faith is *a*, if not *the*, major theme, for at issue above all else is the relationship of human beings to God and to one another as God's creatures. Faith in God is not an immature trust to be outgrown. Rather, the depth of that trust in God can grow, whatever the circumstances of one's life or the lives of God's people.

23

Resilient, maturing faith is our human vocation, yet loss of faith is a tragic human option.

Biblical words for faith in Greek and in Hebrew can be understood as implying two slightly different meanings. One meaning of faith is "trust," as we have just seen. Hebrews 11:1 puts before us a definition of faith as the "assurance of things hoped for, the conviction of things not seen." This kind of faith is trust in the truth, value, and even reality of a God and a future that we cannot see. It is noteworthy that the writer of Hebrews fills chapter 11 with stories of faithful men and women from the Old Testament.

A second meaning for faith is "faithfulness or fidelity." There is overlap between trust and faithfulness in that one abides in faithfulness best when one is in a relationship of trust. But faithfulness to God may be practiced even when trust is nearly gone and God seems absent, unconcerned, or angry. Faithfulness to God has to do with living according to God's covenant promises and God's calling. Paul, for instance, urges the Romans and the Galatians (Rom. 15:13; Gal. 5:5) to remain faithful through the power of the Spirit.

Because of these two similar but distinct shades of meaning, when we look at biblical engagement with the concept "faith," we find several emphases. The first of these is an ongoing deep concern about discerning the true object of faith. A second emphasis is on discernment of how faith in God and/or Christ shapes the life of the believer. Yet a third emphasis is on maintaining this ultimate relationship, that is, on being faithful. All these understandings of faith are richly explored in the Bible.

Before turning to the Bible, we must remind ourselves how many English words are used to translate the Greek and Hebrew words upon which we are focusing. "Faith" in all its forms, including "faithfulness"; "trust" in its forms, including "trustworthy"; "belief" and its forms are all used to translate the same linguistic and conceptual root word. In this chapter, we will interweave all these forms of speaking of faith.

Old Testament

Abraham and Moses

The Bible tells stories. In these stories—told, repeated, interpreted over millennia—we can discern the meaning of words, see patterns of behavior and meaning, glimpse the God who created, maintains, loves, and reaches out to creation and all creatures. Abraham is the first biblical character of whom it is said, "He had faith in God," or better, "He trusted in God" (Gen. 15:6). Since Abraham is the first of the three patriarchs of Israel (Abraham, Isaac, and Jacob), the story of his trust in God is foundational for understanding Jewish and Christian faith. The story of Abraham and God begins in Genesis 12 where Abram (whose name will be changed in 17:5 as part of God's covenant making) is called to leave his homeland and father's house and go to a new land that is not named. This call from God is followed by the promise of blessing for Abram and his descendents. Remarkably, "Abram went, as the LORD had told him" (12:4). This act is not named as faith, but it does show Abram's willingness to trust in God's call and promise. Abram continues in loyalty to God but does not have even one child, let alone the many descendents God promised. It is God's reiteration of that promise as Abram looks into the heavens to count the stars, that maintains Abram's belief. The trust (or belief or faith—all the same word) was reckoned to Abram as righteousness by the Lord. Here surely we can understand Abram's faith as confidence in the Lord. To gaze upon God's creation was to be reminded that the One who had created the vast reaches beyond human ability to number has the power to create human descendents for Abram. Confidence that God could provide an heir was also accompanied by confidence that God would keep that promise to do so. Faith for Abram flowed from his confidence or trust that God had the ability *and* will to keep promises to (be in covenantal relationship with) humankind.

A second significant cluster of terms occurs in Exodus 4 (see vv. 1, 5, 8, 9, and 31), embedded in the story of Moses. Like Abraham, Moses receives a sudden and surprising summons from God.

In the case of Moses, the summons is to leadership of his own people against the mighty empire of Egypt. Given his own complex history, Moses properly wonders how God's people Israel will "believe" him (Exod. 4:1). God transforms Moses' staff into a snake and back again so that "they may believe that the LORD, the God of their ancestors, the God of Abraham, the God of Isaac, and the God of Jacob, has appeared to you" (4:5). God goes on to provide other signs that could convince people that God's power was at work in Moses. After seeing the signs, the people do believe or trust that God has "seen their misery," and they worship God in response (4:31). Again, we might think of the word "confidence" to describe how the people experienced Moses' witness to God's good purpose. They believed both that God could wield the power most clearly demonstrated in God's control of creation *and* they believed that God would use that power on their behalf. We can see in this story that memory played an important role as well. That God had "given heed to the Israelites and . . . seen their misery" meant that God was keeping the covenant promises made so long ago to Abraham, Isaac, and Jacob. Believing or having faith in the God of the patriarchs meant recalling promises and trusting that God remained in covenant with them, in spite of how they may have despaired. To believe in God is not only to believe that God is, but more importantly, to believe (have faith) that God is trustworthy and faithful.

The stories of Abraham and Moses became part of Israel's confession of faith in God in Deuteronomy 26:7–9. Such convictions about God shape Israel's life even—or perhaps especially—when God seems absent. Warned that they will be faithless (not trusting in God), Israel is given the possibility of repentance and returning to faith over and over again because God is faithful (Deut. 30:1–6; 32:4). Faith in terms of being reliable, keeping promises, and being trustworthy is characteristic of God. Faith in terms of confidence in those promises, loyalty to covenant, and trust is to be characteristic of God's people. Although human doubts about God's faithfulness sometimes play out in faithlessness among people, God is not faithless. That is, God is reliably the God of and for Israel: God does not renege on covenants with Abraham, Moses, or David.

The Psalms: Israel's Faith in Song

In the Psalms, those hymns of worship that show us Israel's heart, God's faithfulness is proclaimed, thus allowing Israel to rejoice and to confess infidelity in confident hope of forgiveness. Psalm 106 rehearses the story of God's delivery of the people from Egypt, connecting their belief (faith, trust) to the destruction of their enemies in the Red Sea (106:12). Their faith was quickly forgotten and the people are said to have had "no faith in his [God's] promise" (106:24). The confession of Israel's faithlessness escalates in descriptions of loss of identity as God's people, worship of idols, and even the sacrifice of their children to idols. The confession, however, moves on to proclaim God's faithfulness in slightly different vocabulary. God "remembered his covenant" and "showed compassion" because of God's "steadfast love." All these are definitions of God's faithfulness.

For a similar use of the exodus story and the faithlessness of the people to a God who had saved them, see Psalm 78. Particularly poignant is the statement that God's "anger mounted against Israel, because they had no faith in God, and did not trust his saving power." One half of the sentence interprets the other half; lack of trust in God's saving power is the definition of having no faith. Nonetheless, the psalmist goes on to say, God rained manna from heaven, the very "grain of heaven" (78:22–24). In a word, God remained faithful to his promise to save this people.

Psalm 89 rejoices in the covenant God made with David (2 Sam. 7:8–16). The fact that "faithfulness surrounds" God makes the psalmist's plea possible. This faithfulness, God's keeping of promises made (Ps. 89:8, 14), creates confidence in king and in the well-being of the people. The psalmist claims that David was faithful also to God (v. 19). Here a faithful relationship is the foundation of confidence and hope. David manifests his faithfulness in response to God's faithful presence in identifying God as "Father" and "Rock of my salvation."

This psalm raises the tension between punishment and faithful love. The psalmist declares that God will punish those who violate God's commands (vv. 30–32). Even as God punishes, however, the psalmist boldly reminds God of those promises made to David, promises in accord with the exultant description of God at the beginning of the psalm. God will not gainsay God's own faithfulness to covenant promises or the steadfast love that God has promised (vv. 33–34). Punishment can neither extinguish the people nor last forever. It is important that punishment does not impugn faithfulness of God; yet experiences of defeat and shame have made the psalmist wonder why God delays so long. The plea to God in this psalm, the plea to come to the aid of king and people, is based on the faithfulness of God, that is, God's reliable loyalty to promises made.

In Psalm 116:10, we see how "faith" implies a content and comes to be understood as a particular body of belief. This is a slightly different understanding than faith as a relationship of trust. In this case, the psalmist has been suffering deeply and is led to pray, "O LORD, save my life" (116:4). The psalmist, delivered from death by God, remembers that he "kept [his] faith" even in the midst of dreadful affliction (v. 10). Keeping one's faith, here to be understood as remaining confident in the character of God as revealed in Israel, is a strong, positive claim to make. The psalmist recognizes that God has particular care for God's faithful ones (v. 15) to protect and benefit them. The responsive relationship of faith in or faithfulness that humans have with a faithful God is of inestimable value. The simple and profound statement, "I believe [that is, have faith] that I shall see the goodness of the LORD in the land of the living" is a description of human faithfulness (Ps. 27:13).

Psalm 111:7–8 provides a concise vision of the faithfulness of God and the faithful human response. The entire psalm praises the Lord in the midst of the assembly. The psalm is truly a hymn or liturgical experience of the body of Israel, offered by a community. It proclaims the qualities of the Lord, which elicit praise. His work and his deeds are wonderful, full of honor, and the like because of who God is. It is the Lord's mercy, grace, and mindfulness of covenant (111:5) that make his works also "faithful and just" (v. 7). God's precepts, the congregation sings, are also "trustworthy," because God is trustworthy, loyal, and just. For humans, those precepts are to be faithfully carried out (v. 8). It is the appropriate response to being in covenant with God, a covenant that will last "forever." One can readily see how God's faithfulness flows from God's being and how human faithfulness to this trustworthy partner and the precepts that are in accord with God's character and will flows from recognition of God's being.

The Prophets Call Israel to Keep Faith

This dual faith, that of God in keeping faith with God's promises, including the covenants with Israel, and that of Israel in trusting and obeying God, moves into the intertestamental period and the New Testament as well. This relational understanding of faith, trust, and faithfulness undergirds the nuances this group of words comes to have over time. When one trusts God, for instance, one believes what God has said. This belief in God is eventually applied on occasion to belief about God. Such belief can be tested. Continuing in belief or perseverance can be another understanding of faith. Compare the American idiom "Keep the faith."

In the book of the prophet Isaiah, an important verse may show this sense of faith: "If you do not stand firm in faith, you shall not stand at all" (Isa. 7:9). Perseverance in belief and/or trust in God are at issue in this verse as God speaks to Ahaz through the mouth of Isaiah. The prophet speaks, as the prophets so often do in the Bible, of the failure of Israel (as a whole or embodied in the leaders) to abide in faithfulness to God. The work of the prophets is to call Israel and warn the people of what their turning aside from faith will mean. The turning aside can be a turning toward other gods in worship, a failure to serve the neighbor, or ignoring justice in market and palace. Faithlessness to God can be blasphemy, apostasty, idolatry, or unjust treatment of the neighbor. Faithlessness in these situations consists in ignoring God's character as determinative for how things really are.

New Testament

As Christians began to develop their own identity and commitments, "faith" in God as revealed in Jesus of Nazareth, crucified and raised, became central to their self-understanding. Those early disciples of Jesus, all Jews, knew that faith in God, keeper of ancient promises, was the hallmark of their community and tradition. Jews were called to trust that God would keep those ancient promises to Abraham, Moses, and, especially perhaps, to David. As belief spread among non-Jews that Jesus was indeed the Messiah through whom the blessings of the Holy Spirit were poured out, these Gentiles began to form the larger percentage of early Christian gatherings. Jews and Gentiles alike turned to Scripture (our "Old" Testament) to understand how the promises of a faithful God had been realized in Jesus and would now include peoples never before in relationship with the God of the Jews. How could God be faithful if God's own people did not receive the blessings given by the resurrected Jesus?

The questions of God's faithfulness and human faith are centrally at issue in these earliest texts of Christian communities struggling to discern what God had done in Jesus' death and resurrection. How would the worship and blessing of Gentiles be consistent, if not continuous, with the deepest, most cherished understandings of God? Given the importance of Abraham as a man of faith in God and also as ancestor of Israel, it should not surprise us to find arguments about God's faithfulness and human faith taking shape around understandings of his story.

Paul and Faith

Paul, our earliest New Testament writer, gives a great deal of attention to Abraham in Romans 4 and Galatians 3. In Romans 4, Paul reflects on Genesis 15:6, where Scripture tells us that "Abraham believed [had faith in, trusted] the LORD; and the LORD reckoned it to him as righteousness." According to Paul, Abraham's faith, reckoned as righteousness, preceded the giving of the sign of circumcision and preceded the giving of the law (see Gal. 3:6–29). Faith, therefore, is not about faithfulness in keeping the law as an expression of God's character and will. Faith is a complete trust in God's promise keeping. This trust was exemplified for Paul in Abraham's continuing faith that God would provide numerous descendents, even though Abraham was long, long past the age for fathering children (Rom. 4:21). Paul insists that Scripture itself commends such radical trust as core to one's identity as part of God's people. The death and resurrection of Jesus, received by faith, mark the justification or reconciliation of humans and God, including peoples who do not adhere to the law as set forth in Scripture. As Abraham's faith preceded the law and justified him, so now, those who are children of Abraham by living with the same kind of trust in God revealed in Jesus are justified.

Paul's arguments are complex and engage Scripture in ways no longer common. Paul must make strong arguments to claim that Abraham's faith is that which made him "father" to those who trust God. Abraham as a trusting servant of God who, according to the Jews, obeyed the law written "on his heart" before it existed, was their most important ancestor. If God were to be trustworthy, it must be seen that God did not simply break covenant with Abraham or David. Rather, the understanding of that covenant had to be redefined to include non-law-keeping folks. Faith became the fulcrum for leveraging non-Jewish Christians into the people of God.

The Evangelists Connect God's Covenant Promises to Jesus
Matthew therefore claims right up front in his Gospel (Matt. 1:1) that Jesus is son of David and Abraham. In Luke's Gospel, Mary and Zechariah connect the births of their sons Jesus and John to God's promise to Abraham and his descendents (Luke 1:55, 73). Jesus is the savior that the faithful God now brings forward, as so long ago promised. John's Gospel makes the most lengthy and explicit argument about who really is a child of Abraham and what that might mean. One cannot miss the signal importance of Abraham's faith in Genesis 15 as central to Christian claims to be faithful without the law. Faith, then, has to do with trust in God and "hope in things unseen."

In other sections of the New Testament, faith also refers to the body of belief itself. Ephesians 4:4–6, which proclaims that there is one body, one Spirit, and one hope, insists that there is also "one Lord, one faith," and the like. This "one faith" describes the belief that Jesus is son of God in whose name Christians are baptized and through whom salvation is given. The Letter of James offers a great debate about the importance and even the essence of faith. Sounding like an Old Testament prophet, James asks how acts of injustice can possible cohere with faith (Jas. 2:1). With such a question, James makes it clear that faith must be more than a matter of words about belief or trust but must be woven into all of one's life. "Even the demons," James says, "believe—and shudder" (2:19). For James, assent to God's power revealed in Jesus Christ may be a kind of faith, but it is not a life of faith. James looks for coherence between confession and practice.

Reflections

Faith's centrality as a fruit of the Spirit that defines human relationships with God (Gal. 5:22) takes on a variety of nuances in the New Testament as well as the Old. Trust in God as powerful and as a faithful promise-keeper from and into eternity undergirds other understandings. Human faith can be understood as faithfulness and obedience to God's revealed will (revealed in Scripture, in Jesus himself, or through the Holy Spirit). It can mean persevering in such faith, even in times of trouble. It can mean a dependence on God alone for hope, peace, and salvation. It can mean trusting that God will do as God has promised. All of these are similar, yet each has its own emphasis. All these meanings can be and have been discerned in the same group of words, in the same stories of the faith. Over the millennia in which humans have been called to ponder and to act, to shape their lives on their relationship with God, faith has been a key to describing the relationship and the character of the God by whom we have been addressed.

Questions for Discussion

1. Brainstorm as many different synonyms for "faith" or "faithful" as you can. Which ones seem most important to you? How might you understand these forms of "faith" as biblical?
2. What does it mean in a marriage ceremony that a couple promises to be faithful? How might the many biblical understandings of faith enrich this marital commitment?
3. Read Psalm 33:1–11 (especially vv. 6 and 10) and discuss its portrayals of faithfulness. Explore what the life of the faithful might look like, how the faithful engage God, and when.
4. In the Old Testament and the New, faith is a quality of God, individuals, and communities. What might a faithful community look like in our time? What advantages and/or disadvantages are there when we understand faith as a quality of community?

Chapter Four

Forgiveness

Forgive us our debts, as we also have forgiven our debtors.
                                                    Matt. 6:12

The Greek and Hebrew words often translated in English Bibles as "forgive" can also mean to let go, to carry for someone, to abandon. They can also mean to remit a debt, a use with strong commercial and legal overtones, or to free a horse or a prisoner. The surprisingly elasticity of "forgive" should be in the forefront of our thinking as we engage the biblical texts in this chapter and then, through them, our own world. We will see that this kind of elasticity, this loosening of bonds, is seen as a definitive part of who God is. Since God's character and behavior always have implications for God's people, this word requires our attention.

Old Testament

Two Stories from Genesis

Two wonderful stories from Genesis show us that forgiveness is a reliable trait of God and God's people. Even Pharaoh believes that God forgives the repentant. He dares to plead, quite falsely, for forgiveness, and he receives it (Exod. 10:17). In another story where forgiveness of non-Israelites is at stake, Abraham argues with God in a dialogue that is singular and unforgettable (Gen.

34

18:16–33). God plans to destroy Sodom and Gomorrah for their grave sins about which God has heard outcry. God plans to investigate these two cities before punishing them to be sure that such punishment is warranted and just. Abraham questions whether it is ever just for God to destroy cities, be they ever so sin ridden, if it means destroying righteous persons. Abraham calls God as "Judge of all the earth" (18:25) to do what is just, which in this case means to forgive the sinful in order not to punish unjustly the righteous: "And the LORD said, "If I find at Sodom fifty righteous in the city, I will forgive the whole place for their sake" (18:26). As the story goes, God finally agrees to forgive the city for the sake even of ten. "Forgive" in this story (vv. 24 and 26) means to back off punishment, let the cities go, even though they deserve (and later receive) destruction.

Three principles are taken for granted as true by Abraham and God. One is that God is indeed both just and the judge of all creation. (One could imagine an unjust judge in charge, a fearsome possibility.) Secondly, God's behavior and character or reputation should be consistent. That is, there is no respect for a God who says one thing and does another. Finally, God willingly engages in dialogue, responds to petitions, and even changes God's original intention in conversation with a human who seeks forgiveness for others and courageously reminds "the Judge of all the earth" of appropriate behavior!

In Genesis 50 we see a human display of forgiveness. Joseph had been so despised by his brothers that he was sold as a slave in Egypt. There he rose to prominence by God's grace. After their father's funeral all the brothers are together without their father's mediating presence among them. The brothers are rightly frightened of Joseph, who has both cause for anger and the power to punish. Because the brothers are too scared to plead on their own account for forgiveness, they declare it their father's dying wish that Joseph forgive them. What needs forgiveness is their terrible wrong (Gen. 50:17). Joseph weeps that they ask. They offer to be his slaves, as a kind of restitution or punishment. Joseph's response is telling for us—and will find great play also in the New

Testament: "Am I in the place of God?" God is the one who holds persons accountable. It is not the place of Joseph, exemplary as he may have been, to hold his brothers accountable. He forgives.

Moses: Mediator of Forgiveness

The repentant unrighteous may be forgiven. In Exodus 32, Moses is on the mountain with God while most of Israel, fearing that Moses is gone for good, turns to idolatry. The people create a golden calf, wanting a God who is visible and reliably present, unlike the God "like a devouring fire on the top of the mountain" (Exod. 24:17). Moses finds himself between the people, who have abandoned God, and God, who plans to "consume them" (32:10). Moses, like Abraham before him, pleads with God, reminding God of his reputation with the Egyptians and of the promises made to Israel's ancestors. God then changes God's mind (32:14). Moses himself, when he sees the idolatry in the camp, understands God's rage. But he goes bravely to God again, seeking forgiveness for the people and insisting that he not be kept alive if God plans to destroy everyone else (32:31–32). Again God forgives, but promises punishment at some later date. Here God's forgiveness lies in not destroying everyone who deserves it and in staying with the people as their God. Forgiveness does not always remove all the consequences of wrongdoing.

The people repent, and God agrees to accompany Israel in its journey. When Moses returns to the mountain to receive the commands of the Lord, the Lord begins with self-description (Exod. 34:6–7). God is the one who forgives "iniquity and transgression and sin, yet by no means" simply clears "the guilty." "Forgive" and "remit every consequence" are not synonymous. What, then, is it to forgive? At the very least, to forgive is not to withdraw one's presence, not to hold a grudge, not to seek vengeance, not to shame people with their evildoing. For instance, one might be forgiven careless driving that resulted in a death, yet the consequences remain. So important is this self-description of God that it is woven into many Old Testament books (see Deut. 31; Ps. 103:8–14; Jer. 4:2; 32:18). God's forgiveness in all these locations is God's sticking with the covenant and covenant people. In Numbers 14:19, the prayer is raised, "Forgive the iniquity of this people according to the greatness of your steadfast love, just as you have pardoned this people, from Egypt even until now." The prayer remembers the long history of God's love and the people's long history of needing pardon for their failures. God continues to be in covenant with Israel.

Seeking Forgiveness
God's covenant with Israel offers assurance of forgiveness for people who have sinned consciously or inadvertently. Written into the community-shaping instructions in Leviticus (and repeated in Numbers) are words about forgiveness. Depending upon economic status and intentional or unintentional sin, certain sacrifices were ordered, providing confidence of forgiveness (Lev. 4:20, 26, 31, 35; 5:10, 13, 16, 18; 6:7; 19:22). God had provided for communication of repentance and forgiveness.

Aware of the ongoing need for having sins "let go," Solomon's prayer at the dedication of the first temple speaks repeatedly of God's forgiveness, and pleads in advance for God to continue to forgive the people (see 1 Kgs. 8:30, 34, 36, 39, 50, and 2 Chron. 6:21, 25, 27, 29, 30, and 39). These pleas for forgiveness clarify for what kind of behaviors it would be needed. He prays for God's attentive presence whenever people in duress "stretch out their hands toward this house [the temple]." Solomon's prayer acknowledges that "there is no one who does not sin" (1 Kgs. 8:46) and pleads nonetheless for compassion for those who repent.

A profound prayer of confession, made in hope that God, "who brought your people out of the land of Egypt with a mighty hand," might forgive appears in Daniel 9 (see especially vv. 9 and 17–19). Synonyms of "forgive" include "let your face shine upon your desolated sanctuary" and "listen and act and do not delay." It is noteworthy that Daniel makes his plea to God on the basis of God's mercy and so that God's name not be dishonored. He is clear that "we do not present our supplication before you on the ground of our righteousness." This kind of clarity is interwoven throughout the Old Testament in psalms, prayers, instructions, and stories. It suggests a model for intrahuman as well as God-human communication in relationships where failure is all but inevitable.

Understanding Forgiveness

Forgiveness is also important within Israel's wisdom tradition. In Sirach, a book much read and copied among Jews and early Christians, there are several references. In Sirach 5:6 there is a warning against presuming on God's mercy in order to avoid repentance. Sirach 5:5–8 sounds like many psalms but also like some speeches of Jesus and Paul that will come two centuries later. "Do not be so confident of forgiveness that you add sin to sin," the wise teacher says, very much as Paul writes to the Romans in 6:1, "Should we continue in sin in order that grace may abound?" Consciously sinning with an arrogance about God's will to forgive is an evil in and of itself. As both Paul and Sirach point out, God is mighty to forgive and yet does know wrath (against injustice and idolatry). In Sirach 28 (sounding like Matt. 6:12 and Mark 11:25), one is called upon to forgive the neighbor a wrong done; then one's own sins will be pardoned. "Does anyone harbor anger against another, and expect healing from the Lord?" Sirach asks. In these verses forgiveness is akin to pardon, not being vengeful, having mercy, not being angry. Here is an example of God's behavior as a model for human behavior. In addition, hypocritical requests for forgiveness are skewered. Hypocrisy happens when one seeks forgiveness but does not forgive. It also is hypocritical to seek forgiveness of God, even by the God-given means of Leviticus, all the while persisting in injustice (Sir. 34:23–31). If the sacrifice is properly offered but has been unjustly taken from the poor, the needy, or the employee, there is no forgiveness. These are important verses whose content is picked up often in the parables and stories of Jesus.

New Testament

Our New Testament study begins with various epistles and with a second surprise. "Forgive" is found infrequently. Paul has often been thought to be greatly interested in forgiveness of sins, but in

Paul's authentic letters we find only five occurrences of the Greek word *aphiemi*, which is usually translated "forgive." Only one of these, Romans 4:7, refers to forgiveness and is a quotation of Psalm 32 in which the psalmist points out the blessedness of those "whose iniquities are forgiven." This is a useful psalm because two other phrases are in parallel with "iniquities are forgiven"— namely, "sins are covered" and "will not reckon sin." Paul quotes this psalm and reminds the Romans that blessedness comes as one trusts in God. Forgiveness is necessary for any relationship. The one who trusts God is blessed in the reception of it. Paul's other uses participate in that elasticity of the word and refer to "divorce" (i.e., "let go") in 1 Corinthians 7:11–13 and simply "give up" or "let go" in Romans 1:27.

This word is not at the center of Paul's thought about human relationships with God. Paul's argument turns much more on the questions of how people are "justified" or "made righteous/just" in the eyes of God. This is especially important for the Gentiles, who have not had means to participate in the practices of repentance and atonement available to Jews. Paul insists that such atonement has been made for them through Jesus and that the Holy Spirit empowers them to live a new life. This is a way of thinking and talking about forgiveness that has moved into somewhat new territory. The lives of whole peoples are at stake.

The Gospels: About Forgiveness

Christians tend to remember a number of Jesus' sayings on forgiveness as characteristic of him. "Forgive seventy times seven times." "Father, forgive them." "Forgive us our trespasses/debts/sins." A third surprise is that the theme of forgiveness is not frequently mentioned in the Gospels or Acts. Indeed, there is one use of "forgiveness" in John's Gospel: near the Gospel's end Jesus grants the power to forgive or retain sins to his disciples who have received the Holy Spirit. Matthew, Mark, and Luke give us more to chew on. All three give us John the Baptist, who comes to proclaim a baptism of repentance for the forgiveness of sins, a concept abundantly familiar from Jewish Scripture (Matt. 3:1–11; Mark 1:4; Luke 3:3). All three describe John as a prophet. They quote Scripture (another prophet, Isaiah) to describe John as the prophet whose coming heralds a time when God's paths shall be made straight (Matt. 3:3; Mark 1:3; Luke 3:4) and "all flesh shall see the salvation of God" (Luke 3:6). John's calling had been foretold. His role is to "give knowledge of salvation to his people by the forgiveness of their sins" (Luke 1:77). In other words, the relation with God will be restored and people will be able to trust God again. In Matthew, John's preaching is connected to the nearness of the kingdom of heaven, a state synonymous with salvation and the presence of God. The actual phrase "forgiveness of sins" does not appear in Matthew until near the end, at the Last Supper, where Jesus speaks of the wine as "my blood of the covenant, which is poured out for many for the forgiveness of sins" (Matt. 26:28). Neither Mark nor Luke uses this phrasing at the Last Supper, but Luke's Jesus does tell his disciples that they will proclaim "repentance and forgiveness of sins . . . to all nations" (Luke 24:47). Forgiveness of sins is for restoration of relationship with God, now for all. Jesus is seen as "God's communication system" that all may know themselves as God's people.

The combination of words "proclaim . . . release" appears in Luke 4:18, where Jesus reads a passage from Isaiah to describe his own ministry. "Release" is the same word as "forgiveness," but the presence of the phrase "to the captives" makes it hard to translate as "forgiveness." We must understand these two phrases, one at the beginning of Jesus' ministry and one at the end, as similar. "Release" for the captives is release from whatever it is that separates them from God. Did their sins or the sins of others separate them from God and destroy their hopes? Those sins will be forgiven and the captives, like the poor, oppressed, and blind, will enjoy the year of the Lord's favor. Jesus makes this prophecy his own. He will release captives held by the consequences of sin—their own and that of others.

The Gospels: Stories of Forgiveness

Jesus speaks of the forgiveness of sins in a number of stories that Matthew, Mark, and Luke have in common. These stories center on the power and authority to forgive sins and create *shalom* (wholeness/wellness/salvation), an activity of God in the Old Testament. Mark presents a dramatic scene of forgiveness very early in his Gospel when Jesus is in Capernaum with a huge crowd of persons seeking to be healed (Mark 2:1–12; Luke 5:17–26; Matt. 9:1–8). One paralyzed man is lowered through the roof by the friends who brought him to Jesus, for whose sake Jesus declares the paralytic's sins forgiven. When the local religious authorities wonder silently (in Mark's version) if Jesus is arrogating to himself power belonging only to God, Jesus heals the paralytic so that he is able to rise and carry his own mat home. The healing is a sign of Jesus' power over all that separates humans from God, illness, and sin. Mark puts the story early in Jesus' ministry in order to establish Jesus' authority and make clear that the authority is from God. Forgiving sins is a way of speaking of establishing relationship with God. In Leviticus even unwitting sins could be repented of and forgiven as part of the communication between God and humankind. Here Jesus restores that relationship.

Matthew and Luke also reflect on forgiveness in a dialogue between Peter and Jesus (Matt. 18:21–22; Luke 17:3–4). Because Peter is such an important character, we know that these few verses are significant. Peter asks Jesus, "How often should I forgive?" The two Gospel writers differ on Jesus' math a bit, but neither answer (seventy-seven in Matthew or seven times in one day in Luke) is to be taken literally. According to Luke's Jesus, one forgives every time a disciple repents. Matthew does not even mention the qualification of repentance. Instead of a number (how many times?), Jesus indicates that those who follow him are forgivers, just as he is. One thinks back to Sirach's warning not to expect healing or good from God if we are unwilling to forgive but instead harbor anger. Forgiving, then, is about not harboring anger or a grudge but leaving recompense to God (remember Joseph in Gen. 50). Forgiving does not mean putting oneself in harm's way repeatedly or feigning amnesia about evil that has been done. There are consequences to bad behavior, but punitive anger, resentment, and dehumanization are not called for.

Matthew and Luke each also offer an additional parable about forgiveness. Matthew's parable follows the dialogue between Peter and Jesus (Matt. 18:23–35). The parable illustrates the expectation that fellow slaves forgive each other their relatively petty debts, just as a king forgives huge debts. The act of forgiveness is characterized in this parable as "forgiving debt," "having mercy," and "releasing" (Matt. 18:27, 33). The final line in the parable brings the story directly to Jesus' audience. God will treat humans with the same unforgiving harshness as they treat one another. This strong language could come straight from Sirach, where forgiveness among humans is an issue. Luke's parable, in which forgiveness is particularly mentioned, reverses the dynamic of Matthew's and contends that the one who shows the greatest love is the one who has been forgiven most (Luke 7:36–50). In this remarkable story we do not know the nature of the sin forgiven, but we watch Jesus reframe the woman's actions as an outpouring of gratitude for forgiveness. The last line in this parable connects her trust in Jesus, her forgiveness, and her wholeness, set over against the internal resentment and suspicion of Jesus that animated Simon.

Forgiveness in the Lord's Prayer

When Jesus is asked to teach his disciples a prayer, he includes both petition and promise of forgiveness of sins (Matt. 6:9–14; Luke 11:2–4). The phrases of the Lord's Prayer, as it has come to be called, could be prayed by Jews, as indeed they are within the Gospel narratives. Matthew's and Luke's prayers are remarkably similar, offering a vision of life as God would have it lived (God's kingdom on earth as in heaven). People pray for enough food, safety from trials of the evil one (or evil), and forgiveness. Matthew specifies that debts are what are to be forgiven; Luke speaks of sins. Both evangelists highlight that we have failed to "pay" what is owed to God—whether literally (offerings, tithes) or more figuratively (honor, gratitude, love). The prayer pleads for these debts to be forgiven, that is, let go, not held against us. It likewise states that we do forgive those indebted to us—again literally or figuratively. Matthew adds a warning at the end of his prayer in verse 14: Forgiveness must be mutual. You cannot refuse to forgive others and expect God to forgive you. The mutuality of forgiveness is emphasized in all three Gospels. Mark includes a similar statement, although not connected to the Lord's Prayer. In Mark 11:25, Jesus instructs the disciples about prayer, encouraging them to pray for their heart's desire and to trust that they will receive it. However, Jesus also says that one is called to pray unimpeded by holding a grudge against anyone: Forgive, resolve your anger *so that* God may forgive you.

Disciples Mediate Forgiveness

As the disciples witness to Jesus as Messiah in the book of Acts, forgiveness of sins is used to summarize Jesus' activity. Peter sounds like John the Baptist when he calls upon his hearers to "repent, and be baptized . . . so that your sins may be forgiven" (Acts 2:38). Peter, however, makes two additions: people are now baptized in the name of Jesus Messiah, and they receive the Holy Spirit at baptism. In preaching about Jesus, Peter insists that God exalted Jesus to God's right hand so that he "might give repentance to Israel and forgiveness of sins" (5:31). Peter roots these events in the words of the prophets (Scripture as a whole), much as we have done. Jesus, in a word, is God's power for forgiveness made real, vivid, present; he both signifies and enables the end of separation from God and of unjust treatment of the neighbor. This great privilege is offered to Gentiles in Acts 10:43 and newly to Jews without the requirements of the processes we saw in Leviticus (Acts 13:38). When Paul looks back on his own calling, he also remembers that Jesus commanded him to preach forgiveness (26:18). Paul is to open the eyes of Jews and Gentiles "so that they may receive forgiveness of sins and a place among those who are sanctified by faith in me." Acts clarifies the big shift in all New Testament writings: God has begun also to call the Gentiles to faith in God and a life in which they are not captive to sin or without hope.

Reflections

Forgiveness is an important element in the relationship of God and humankind as well as among people themselves. Because it was God's desire to forgive and thus maintain relationship with God's people, God provided Israel with ways to seek forgiveness and experience confidence in having received it. Jesus of Nazareth became the way to seek and know forgiveness for millions not of Israel and for many within. God was never interested in "cheap forgiveness." Reminded by Wisdom literature, by all the prophets, and by Jesus, we hear that it is wrongheaded and wrong-hearted to expect God to forgive us when we do not forgive or are otherwise unjust to our neighbors. Our request for forgiveness from God cannot rely on a formula, as if God were able to be programmed to forgive on demand. We are challenged to set aside anger or vindictiveness even as we yearn to live at peace with God. God summons us to ongoing discernment of our participation in God's creation here and now as part of our faith.

Questions for Discussion

1. How would you explain the difference between forgiveness and reconciliation?
2. In contemporary society we have come to understand forgiveness as a cognitive or psychological act. The Bible seems to understand forgiveness as more about behavior. Are there ways that the biblical view might help us forgive?
3. Forgiving is one expectation for Christians. Receiving forgiveness is another and perhaps more difficult one. What is involved in receiving forgiveness? What makes it difficult? What makes it a blessing?
4. What does it look like in contemporary terms to forgive someone, while not taking away the consequences of evil or criminal behavior?

Chapter Five

Hope

Let your steadfast love, O LORD, be upon us, even as we
hope in you.

Ps. 33:22

To hear "hope" echoing through the stories of God's people,
one must do more than listen sharply for just one particular
word. Both Hebrew and Greek have a word most often translated
as "hope," but there are many additional terms that express that
same posture of looking to the future expectantly. Consider the
hope inherent in "waiting" or "awaiting" the Lord, in "longing
for" and "watching for" that day of the Lord when justice and
peace may kiss one another (Ps. 85:10). Hope is a way of imagining God's future and persevering in faith that it will arrive. Hope
is a way of imagining God and persevering in relationship until
"we see face to face" (1 Cor. 13:12). Hope is about the "day of the
Lord," the "then," the "not yet" for which God's people have
longed. As we become better acquainted with this theme of hope
in the Bible, we will pay attention to three particular aspects of it:

the object of hope (for what does one hope?)
the grounds for one's hope (on what basis does one hope?)
the conditions in which one hopes (when does one hope?)

Old Testament

When God interacts with humans, there is always surprise involved. No one can predict the presence, the message, the action of a fully sovereign deity who is not visible in our human dimension. The Bible, however, begins the story of God and humankind by insisting on God's covenant-making behavior. God speaks with Adam and Eve, with Noah, Abraham, Moses, and David, among others, to establish a relationship with humankind. God's speech also reveals God's own characteristics: fidelity, steadfast love, mercy, and righteousness. God's word was written for Israel in the circumcision of the flesh, on stone tablets, and in the Torah. Part of Israel's confident hope is that one day God's will and voice will also be written on hearts, will become a part of who each person is, so that we will walk in God's ways and the world will be a place of *shalom* (see Jer. 31:33). Our exploration of hope in the Old Testament is divided into two parts. First, we will turn to the stories that help us see "hope," and second, we will look at the psalms as the worshipful expressions of Israel's hope in God.

Seeing Hope

Toward the end of Genesis, Jacob, who is dying, gathers his sons and predicts their future. In Genesis 49:18, he interrupts his list with a one-verse confession of hope: "I wait for your salvation, O LORD." This confession on behalf of his sons and of all Israel is perfectly at home in Jacob's long speech, for it is within the lives of people in the future that God's salvation will be known. Jacob's statement shows his confidence that God will indeed save, that God will be faithful to God's covenant people, and that the future is not yet. To wait is to hope, for without hope one would cease to wait. One would give up. "I wait for your salvation, O LORD" expresses hope clearly. We will hear it again and again.

Isaiah, in the midst of political and military turmoil that has driven many in Israel to consult other gods, insists that he will "wait for the LORD" and "hope in him," even though the Lord "is hiding his face from the house of Jacob" (Isa. 8:17). Here it is clear that "hope" and "wait for" are synonymous. Isaiah speaks poetically of such hope, connecting it with yearning, waiting, and trust (26:4, 8, 9). Isaiah's hope is articulated during trying conditions, and it is hope for God's righteousness, justice, and peace. There is both a longing for and a confidence in new life at God's hand (26:19). Such hope is deeply grounded in God's character and the memory of God's acts on behalf of the people (26:8, 12, 15).

Humans can misplace hope. Isaiah is urgently concerned for a people that continue mistakenly to trust and hope in alien rulers and their mighty armies, rather than in God (30:1–14). The prophet warns the people not to trust Egypt's pharaoh to save them but to trust only in the "Holy One of Israel" (30:15–26). Hoping in God's providence is Israel's calling. Israel prays in passionate hope for God's intervention (33:2–6). This prayer articulates the grounding of hope as the "fear of the LORD," "Zion's treasure." The objects of hope are: abundance of salvation, wisdom, knowledge, stability (33:5–6). There is no limit to this hope (59:21). For Isaiah, the failure of hope to be realized can be attributed in some cases to the transgressions of the people. The transgressions themselves "distance" the people from God and from all for which they hope (59:1–15). This conviction suggests that hope is about a very active waiting, a looking forward in accord with God's commands.

One of the most enduring statements of hope in the Old Testament is Isaiah 60–61. Here the end of violence is promised and the presence of God is portrayed as everlasting light. The people themselves shall "all be righteous" (60:21). This presence of God, the prevailing of salvation, righteousness, and joy, is to be accomplished by the Lord. In Isaiah 60:22 comes the word that has nurtured hope among God's people: "I am the LORD; in its time I will accomplish it quickly." In fact, it is this hope the earliest Christians looked for after Jesus' resurrection. His resurrection was evidence that God was "accomplishing" that restoration and salvation so long ago promised.

Jeremiah, in the midst of terrible strife and drought, calls upon God to act in spite of whatever evils the people have done (Jer.

14:7–9). In his prayer, Jeremiah addresses God with a phrase synonymous with his name: "O hope of Israel." Jeremiah continues with another phrase that clarifies what this hope means: Israel's "savior in time of trouble." We see that Israel's confidence in God as promise keeper provides conviction about a future in which there will be peace and plenty. Such hope also appears at the end of the prayer.

Similar calls to "return to God" and "wait continually" for God show up throughout the prophets, determined as they are to steer Israel back onto the path leading to God's future. For language about hope in God's future see Hosea 12:6, Micah 7:7, and Zephaniah 3:8. All of these prophets call upon Israel to wait for God's day, God's future, when God will bring things around right. There are, to be sure, differences among biblical writers about just what it is that God will do in that future. All agree that God will provide salvation to Israel's faithful. What will happen to those either who are unfaithful or who are not of Israel is not always portrayed the same. Overall, however, it can be said that Israel dared to continue to hope in, long for, and await the future provided by a God who was "their" God and for them. That the future seemed so long in coming pressed Israel to wonder why this might be so. The delay of God's future also set the stage for a future "already and not yet" in the New Testament.

Before we turn to later writers who are eager to connect God's future to Jesus, let's look at the psalms. These prayers and hymns were important both to Israel and to the early church as it sought to redefine hope. They continue to be important among churches today. What can we discern about hope from the psalms?

Hope-Filled Singing

Psalm 33:17–22 sets the agenda for thinking clearly about hope. In just a few words this psalm quickly characterizes the God to whom it is raised (vv. 4–5) and makes a clear statement of this God as the only basis for hope. Because the Lord keeps watch on those who "hope in his steadfast love" (v. 18), it is the Lord for whom Israel "waits" (v. 20). Hope in the Lord is hope for deliverance (cf.

Gal. 1:4), not least from hunger and death (Ps. 33:19). Hope is the human side of relationship with God. It expresses a longing for what is cherished and trusted, yet unfulfilled, for what is believed but not yet revealed. Psalm 33 closes with the verse, "Let your steadfast love, O LORD, be upon us, even as we hope in you." The connection of God's steadfast love with human hope shows up beautifully in Psalm 130 also. In verses 5 and 6, the psalmist speaks of waiting for the Lord as watching for the morning. "Wait for" and "watch for" put us in the milieu of hope. In fact, verses 5 and 7 use the word "hope," giving both the reason for it and its outcome. Israel is to hope in the Lord alone, because the Lord has both "steadfast love" for Israel and "great power." God must be both beneficent and have the power to create the future for God to be a ground of hope. The final word? "It is he who will redeem Israel from all its iniquities" (Ps. 130:8).

Instances of hope in the Old Testament abound but do not contain nuances that differ significantly from what we have already seen. As we move into Christian writings, remember that confidence in the future as belonging to God, being brought in by God, and having the theme of steadfast love and covenant promise keeping had some variance in interpretation among Jews. We will see some of that variety emerge also among Christian writers.

New Testament

The New Testament writers continued looking toward God's future, but with a new sense of urgency based on confidence that God's long-promised blessings were being newly shared after the resurrection of Jesus the Messiah. God had acted to extend the covenantal blessings to the Gentiles through the power and presence of God's Holy Spirit. The New Testament writers had somewhat different "takes" on how and when God's future would finally arrive and what life would be like in the meanwhile, but no one doubted that God had acted in Jesus to gather and save God's people. The energy generated by the presence of the Spirit animated renewed hope that God's reign, God's future, was at hand. This hope was preached by John the Baptist and Jesus himself.

Turning to their Scripture, early Christian writers found prophecies to help them understand the experience of their own time. We will look at three distinctive ways in which hope was understood in the first century after Jesus' resurrection and ascension: that of Paul, Luke, and finally John. These do not cover every nuance of hope among New Testament writers, but provide a sense of the breadth and power of Christian hope, as well as the adaptation of hope over time. The central question, put in the mouth of John the Baptist, "Are you the one who is to come, or are we to wait for another?" (Luke 7:19; Matt. 11:2–3), points backward to Israel's hope and forward to a reign of God that Jesus describes and enacts.

Paul: New Hope for All Creation

Paul is the earliest writer in the New Testament. He therefore gives us a glimpse of the earliest expectation experienced in a wide variety of congregations around the Mediterranean. Some of his congregations seemed to be a mixture of believers drawn from Jewish and pagan backgrounds. Some seem to have been almost entirely pagan in origin. In all these congregations Paul preached confidence that they were among God's people chosen for blessing in this life and forever. In 1 Thessalonians, Paul's earliest extant letter, he comforts mourners in the young congregation by reminding them of their hope (1 Thess. 4:13). The hope springs from confidence that God will raise even those who have died before Jesus' return. It is God's ability to do this and God's will to do this that generate hope.

It is hope, along with love and faith, which "abides" in 1 Corinthians 13:13. Faith in God's love is faith in God's love for eternity. From this faith springs hope for life—one's own, that of others, and indeed of the whole creation. Hope is not a new quality for those who trust God. Paul calls upon Abraham in Romans 4:18 as a model of hope in the midst of a condition that offered no hope. Abraham hoped for the future because of faith in God's power and fidelity. He hoped against hope. In this verse hope and faith are so intimately connected that Paul seems to speak of them almost interchangeably. Yet there is a difference. Faith is that very trust that allows hope to survive. The opposite of hope is not "unfaith" but the losing of heart (2 Cor. 4:16). Another word Paul connects with hope is "boldness" (which can also be translated "confidence" or even "freedom"). In 2 Corinthians 3:12, he brings these two ideas together succinctly: "Since, then, we have such a hope, we act with great boldness." The hope to which he refers here seems to be hope that God's Spirit is actively creating a new people of God and a new creation (2 Cor. 5:17).

Paul is convinced that God has acted to save the entire cosmos. God will redeem all that God has made. In Romans 8:22–25, Paul calls upon the lived experience of believers in Rome. We know, he says, that the whole creation is in bondage to decay. All will die; nothing will last; there is nothing we can do to alter this cycle. We humans are no better off than the rest of creation (v. 23). We see this cycle all around us. Paul goes on to what is unseen, namely, hope. Hope believes that God will redeem all of God's creatures, human and nonhuman (vv. 24–25). In the midst of the suffering of the present age, Paul's hope came from trust in God and the great experience of Jesus' resurrection and the Holy Spirit. At last God was turning the endless tide of death and decay. Trust in God's future called humans to turn toward it with positive expectation.

Hope is required because God's future has not yet arrived. We live "at the ends of the ages," in that overlap of time between the old eon and the new (1 Cor. 10:11), and must live by hope. Paul walks a careful line, reminding people that the certainty of God's future changes everything about the way they live in the present, yet insisting that folks continue in their daily lives, abound in love for one another, and take comfort in the midst of sufferings and joys in the hope for salvation. Paul's major treatise on hope can be found in 1 Corinthians 15, where he explores the idea of a resurrected body, insisting that while we cannot know just what a human body raised from death will be, we can trust that it *will* be. Jesus' resurrection is the crucial "first fruits" of God's new creation. It is the source of human hope.

Luke's Gospel

All the Gospels were written at least twenty years after Paul's letters. Hope was undiminished as the early communities multiplied around the Mediterranean world, but it changed from an expectation of Jesus' imminent return (see 1 Cor. 7, for example), to a waiting for a future the timing of whose arrival was less predictable. There is no indication in Paul's surviving letters that he knew the prayer we call the Lord's Prayer. By the time Luke and Matthew wrote their Gospels, this prayer, in slightly different form, was taught to the disciples with a strong encouragement to pray. It is a prayer of hope, for it begins with a plea that God's name be held as holy and that God's "kingdom come" (Luke 11:2). This is a prayer for those among whom the reign of God is hoped for, perhaps tasted, but not fully known.

In Luke's second volume, the Acts of the Apostles, he makes very clear what it is that Christians hope for. One turns to God so that God may wipe out sins (as also in the Lord's Prayer). One also prays that God will "send the Messiah appointed for you, that is, Jesus, who must remain in heaven until the time of universal restoration that God announced long ago through his holy prophets" (Acts 3:20–21). Again, it is clear that Luke looks back to the Scriptures that prophesied restoration. Based on those ancient promises, empowered by the Spirit poured forth by the resurrected Jesus (Acts 2:33), the community lived by hope for that time yet to come. Several examples of Luke's use of Scripture help to identify what it is for which one dares to hope.

For instance, Peter speaks at the time of Pentecost and quotes words both of the prophet Joel and of the psalmist ("David," Acts 2:25) as predicting exactly the events happening in Jerusalem in the presence of the crowd. He begins, "In the last days it will be, God declares, that I will pour out my Spirit upon all flesh" (Acts 2:17, quoting Joel 2:28, 3:1). "The last days" are the great time of God's action, anticipated with yearning even in the time of Joel, the sixth century BCE. The Spirit's presence is confirmation of the coming of "the last days" and the end of the old eon, but Luke clarifies, as we have seen, that the great restoration is not yet complete. Hope is the proper posture for the interim. The first two chapters of Luke's Gospel show us over and over again how hope was renewed among people whose trust in God was strong but whose expectation of God's action in their own lives was low. Elizabeth, Mary, and Zechariah are filled with hope from the Holy Spirit that God is remembering God's covenant promises. Their hope is furthered by Simeon's quotation (also in the power of the Spirit) of a number of verses from Isaiah. Jesus is understood here to represent the "redemption of Israel" (Luke 1:68), which has been long awaited by many, many faithful souls. Note that Anna speaks of this redemption to "all who were looking" (Luke 2:38). This is about hope. Here we see a people turning to Scripture, to the words of the God upon whom they have waited in hope. Simeon warns Mary that many will not see Jesus as the realization of that hope (2:34–35), but that does not diminish the pervasive sense of looking for God's future. Luke and Paul agree that hope is a gift of the Spirit.

The Writings of John

There is only use of the Greek word for "hope" in John's Gospel and in the Johannine letters. This surely does not mean that John's congregations were without hope. Indeed, the very purpose of John's Gospel is that it might create life-giving belief in Jesus as Messiah (John 20:30–31). In this Gospel, Jesus' long speeches give hope for the future of believers no matter what happens. In John 13:31–17:26 Jesus speaks to his disciples, promising peace and the presence of the Spirit of truth (16:13), the Advocate (16:7), who will continue to lead and guide them. The disciples are called to confidence that whatever pains or struggles they experience (15:18–24; 16:20–23, 33; 17:14–16) they belong to Jesus and look forward to complete joy (15:11; 16:24). The disciples are called to "abide" in Jesus and thereby the Father, to keep Jesus' commandments, and to bear much fruit. Their abiding in the vine, their continuing in the flock, to use metaphors of John's construction, is an "already" experience of the future. That this future will not be without travail is made clear by Jesus in this speech. The disciples will have to live by a combination of trust that Jesus' words are true and hope for the eternal life he promises them.

The future is the eternal life that Jesus says he goes to prepare for the disciples. He reminds them that this means he will come again to fetch them so that they will not be separated from him (John 14:2–30). Hope, then, has to do with life in the presence of Jesus and the Father forever. As we have seen, this hope is based on the promises of Jesus and the signs of his power to fulfill his intentions. Although nonbelievers do not see Jesus, the disciples have hope that they will (John 14:18). Jesus' prediction of all that is to come grounds their hope in experience of his prophetic abilities and his love.

For the Johannine communities, fellowship "with the Father and with his Son Jesus Christ" is a reality, but extending the fellowship into the future will complete their joy (1 John 1:3–4). Great confidence that believers are already God's children (1 John 5:19) and already have eternal life (5:11–12) shapes the life of these communities in such a way that "hope" is not a primary category for them. Yet, as we have seen, the future lies in a completeness of joy and the overcoming of the world (understood here as that realm opposed to the ways of God). All is not yet as it will be in God's time, but these communities are called to abide in Jesus' way, to love one another more than to "hope."

Questions for Discussion

1. As the Jews of the Old Testament traditions differed among themselves about what they hoped for, so did the believers of the New Testament. This kind of difference in what we hope for continues today among Jews, among Christians, and between Jews and Christians. Yet we all claim to be children of the God of the Bible. How do you understand these differences? How do one's hopes shape one's behavior in the present and the future?

2. Hope in an imminent return of Jesus has not come to pass in

the way that Paul and other early believers hoped and imagined it would. Many changes have taken place in the world since then. Consider, for instance, that people live at least twice as long as they did in Paul's day. Consider also the development of Islam. What are some ways that the delay of Jesus' return shapes our hope?

3. Do you think that "hope" as a Christian quality contributes to social indifference? Why or why not?

Chapter Six

Joy

You have turned my mourning into dancing; you have taken off my sackcloth and clothed me with joy, so that my soul may praise you.

Ps. 30:11–12

How does the Bible show us joy? Joy is surely beyond happiness, although it is not totally different from it. Joy is of a different quality from jollity or merriment, although some of the qualities of both of these expressions of well-being and mirth can be part of joy. Rather than coming up with a definition, let us invite the Bible to be our guide to joy and, at the end, see where it has brought us. The Bible is an apt guide for this journey, relishing joy as it does. In the Bible joy is a great good for humans, angels, and even God.

Old Testament

Prophetic Promises of Joy
The words of the prophet Joel go back thousands of years to a time before Alexander the Great had left his extensive cultural "footprint" in the Mediterranean world and Israel. Joel's short work is a poem of hope for Israel. Joel knows, however, that hope and joy cannot flourish unless Israel names, acknowledges, and

mourns its sins. In his first chapter, Joel calls upon all the people of Israel to lament the presence of an invader, the failure of the land to produce, and the "withering away" of joy among the people (Joel 1:12). Humans and animals are starving because all the means of food production have been destroyed and because the land itself has failed (1:17–20). In a time of famine and lack of hope, joy and gladness are cut off. Even worship in God's temple no longer brings joy (1:16). But Joel writes to remind his people that God will deliver them. As we have seen, the description of God's character as gracious, merciful, and abounding in love (2:12–13) is a source of hope for the people, hope for a restoration of the necessities of life and joy.

Joy is that experience of gladness, happiness, and enjoyment at the presence of God and God's blessings. It is the people's response to God's abundant provision, itself a sign of God's beneficent presence. When God is present for the people, there is joy. Joy is not for the people alone, however. The land itself, the soil, and the animals are to be glad and rejoice. When God is present, creation interacts as it should, life goes according to God's plan, all is well, and joy is the creation's response (2:21–22). God's people rejoice as God makes provision for abundance. Joel connects God's provision of abundance through natural means, like plenty of rain, with God's faithfulness to Israel (2:23–24). When Israel is starving or beaten in battle or behaving badly, it seems to them and to all the world as if God no longer cares for Israel. So the pouring down of rain is a vindication. Israel's joy is not only in abundance, then, but more importantly in the restoration of right relationship with God.

This connection of a life of enough and more with the praise of God for God's amazing gifts is made clearly in Joel 2:26. There is a great beauty in these verses, where a people's confidence in God's presence and faithfulness (2:27) is honor and joy for them. Through Joel's prophecy, God promises greater joy yet to come. The pouring out of God's spirit on all flesh will happen "afterward" (2:28–29). Here the way is pointed toward a joy whose fullness will not be tasted until the last days or the end times, when the entire cosmos knows the presence of God and God's justice. This great hope, indeed these very words from Joel 2:28–32, became central to Christian understanding of new joy in God's presence centuries later (Acts 2:16–21).

The same connection between right relationship to God and joy is echoed in the final chapter of Lamentations. In Lamentations a litany of grief resulting from sins describes the lives of God's people. The woes include the hardships of simple survival in an occupied land, the painfully arduous life of brutal toil, and the lack of human dignity for women and men. These sorrows are summed up in Lamentations 5:15–16: "The joy of our hearts has ceased; our dancing has been turned to mourning. The crown has fallen from our head; woe to us, for we have sinned." In poetic fashion, each short phrase helps to interpret the other. Dancing, the ancient expression of a joyful heart, has ceased for a people now in mourning. The crown of joy and celebration, as well as the royal crown, no longer mark the heads of joyous people. Their heads are bare, as befits sinners and sufferers. Loss of relationship with God, that is, sin, has led to disgrace and abandonment, the end of joy. Recognition of our human failures, as well as complaints about life's cruelties that we cannot control, is crucial to the return of joy in Joel and in Lamentations, indeed, throughout the Bible.

Isaiah: Prophet of Suffering and Joy

Among the prophets, Isaiah stands out as interested in joy, though he is certainly not the only prophet of joy. Chapter 12 sets a tone early in his long writing. It is a word of promise for the future. In verses 1 and 3 he provides psalmlike language for Israel to speak together to express joy in deliverance. They will affirm God's trustworthiness, God's being *for* them. Israel has been neither forgotten nor despised. Instead, God is in the people's midst, a source of comfort. God's presence with them is an experience of the joy of salvation (Isa. 12:3). The people will be able to sing and shout for joy (Isa. 12:6). The presence of God for Israel is the source of blessing and well-being, that is, salvation. Centuries later Paul will joyfully proclaim this same truth in Romans 8:38–39. It is his great joy that nothing anywhere "will be able to separate us from the love of God." For Paul the love (and presence of God) has been guaranteed and extended "in Christ Jesus our Lord." This is joy.

Let us return to Isaiah. In his writing we find a "dialogue" between God and Israel, as interpreted by the prophet, that speaks of joy, hope, and vocation. In Isaiah 49, Israel speaks of having been called by God to the futile labor of serving God. To add to Israel's struggles, God has given the people the task of being "a light to the nations" in order that all peoples might be saved by God. (This passage became important for Christians to explain Jesus' role for non-Jews.) This is an almost laughable task from Israel's point of view, since their status before all the nations to whom they would be "light" is itself laughable (Isa. 49:7). No matter, says Isaiah. God is faithful and insists that the heavens and the earth will sing for joy. There are witnesses in nature itself to God's faithfulness (v. 11). Though Israel experiences itself as forgotten and therefore laughable (v. 14), God says otherwise. "Look around," God says, "and see that all shall be well." A mother could forget her own child sooner than I could forget you. Everyone, not Israel only, will know that God is Israel's Savior and Redeemer (v. 26). This knowledge, this confidence, and finally this experience of God, Savior and Redeemer, is cause for joy in Israel and throughout the cosmos. Isaiah 51:1–16 repeats these themes. Verse 11 particularly highlights the joy of exiled Israel whom God has saved and sent home. It is significant in this verse that Israel's joy will be everlasting, thus beyond human imagination but within God's promised vision.

Joy in Worship: Experience and Foretaste of God's Presence
Mourning turns into dancing in Psalm 30:11, where the singer expresses great joy in help and healing from God. Sackcloth, a sign of mourning, is taken away by God; clothing of grief is replaced with clothing of joy. The same psalm asserts that God's faithfulness to God's people, God's favor (Ps. 30:5, 9), is a source

of joy. When God is turned away from the people, or vice versa, joy is lost. But such experiences can only be temporary, given God's promised loyalty to the people. This same claim is made in Psalm 31:7, where the psalmist proclaims exultation and rejoicing precisely in God's steadfast love. The psalmist understands the meaning of God's love very realistically: God sees affliction and difficulties and rescues the trusting psalmist from them. The psalms are full of this kind of affirmation of joy in God's saving presence and God's steadfast love, as one might hope to hear in these songs of the people. In Psalm 40, for instance, a combination of thanksgiving and lament that ends in joy offers this same confession of God's faithfulness, steadfast love, and salvation (Ps. 40:10). It ends with an interesting pair of verses in which "all who seek" God are called upon to "rejoice and be glad." All who "love your salvation," say, "Great is the LORD!" Rejoicing is not only for those who have experienced God's blessing in every situation, but even yearning for God and God's love is a source of joy. The psalmist himself ends with a petition for God's prompt deliverance (from difficulties about which we do not know), confident that God "takes thought" for him, though poor and needy.

Psalm 51:10–12, one more example of that deep connection between joy and God's presence, is a beautiful three-part petition to God for three interwoven realities. First the psalmist pleads to be turned toward God: put a new strong spirit within me and make me fully yours, God. The second petition is very similar, praying that God not take away God's holy spirit, which would be the same as depriving the singer of God's presence. Finally, the psalmist sings again for a God-ward spirit and the joy of God's salvation. Being sustained by God's holy spirit willingly, actively, and in a refreshed way is holy (and wholly) joy in God's presence. This joy is expressed energetically in Psalm 149, where worship of God is marked by joy, praise, and music, as Israel "is glad" and "rejoices" in God, who also takes pleasure in Israel. The "faithful ones" (149:1, 5, 9) experience the faithfulness of God (here in victory over those who would harm them), and it fills them with joy expressed in worship, including dancing (149:3).

Joy While We Wait

Ecclesiastes is a book for the interim time, between that full experience of everlasting joy and the present life, which affords occasional glimpses. The writer of Ecclesiastes has tried to live a life in search of happiness or joy. His conviction is that all things come about according to God's design. Human beings, however, are inherently unable either to discern the full design or grasp God's timetable. For humans, then, joy can be found in faithfulness to the work God has given and in the simple pleasures of eating and drinking, also gifts from God. Ecclesiastes 3:12–13 captures this humble trust that God has granted humans a vocation of value and pleasure, as well as the gifts necessary to sustain life—food and drink. Daring to take responsibility for that work which is God's alone deprives us of joy, for such arrogance is inherently frustrating. At the same time, we may find joy in our own work and in the simple pleasures of creaturely life. The writer repeats his convictions in 3:22, 5:18, and 8:15. In 11:8 he encourages his hearers to rejoice in all the days that they live, however many they may be.

In this writing joy is a human response to God's gifts in life, gifts that are evidence of God's investment in the world and God's people. The writer of Ecclesiastes does not assume that he can identify times of blessing and times of trouble as coming from God or some other source. Somehow for him, the awe-filled understanding is that God brings things about in a timely and faithful way that is well beyond human comprehension. The final verses of the final chapter of the Wisdom of Sirach (51:29–30) also sum up this kind of humble attitude of rejoicing in God rather than trying to be God. This joy is connected to a promise, the time of whose fulfillment is a mystery known only to God: "Do your work in good time, and in his own time God will give you your reward."

New Testament

As we move into the New Testament writings, we will find all these themes repeated and reinterpreted according to the new "clock" set in motion by the death and resurrection of Jesus. Joy in God's presence, joyful confidence in God's commitment to save all creation, the ability of creation itself to rejoice—all these were restored by the empty cross and the presence of the Spirit. Finding joy in humility springs anew from human inability to "figure out" a God whose only son died on a cross.

Luke's Gospel of Joy

It is no accident that early Christians understood that Isaiah and the Psalms prophesied the truths known through Jesus' resurrection and the blessings of the spirit: joy of God's presence, blessing, and deliverance from all enemies, even death. Luke-Acts makes particular use of Isaiah and, not coincidentally, uses more language of joy than the other Gospel writers. In fact, Luke's Gospel begins and ends with words of joy, creating a joyful frame around the entire story of Jesus. The first speech of the angel Gabriel to Zechariah, the first words from God in the Gospel, promise joy: "You will have joy and gladness, and many will rejoice at his birth" (Luke 1:14). Three times joy is heralded. God ushers in times of joy with this child. The unborn John expresses joy in his mother's womb in recognition of Jesus, who is also unborn (1:44), and Mary declares her own rejoicing in God (1:47). What is the cause of all this joy? It is the sudden, but not unexpected, promise of a savior, a prince of peace. It is pure delight and satisfaction—joy, in a word—that God has remembered God's age-old covenants with Israel. It is hope that "we, being rescued from the hands of our enemies, might serve him without fear" (Luke 1:74). Joy springs up when God's faithfulness and God's mercy appear on the scene.

Luke's Gospel ends in a way similar to its beginning. At the beginning, Zechariah is in the temple serving God when Gabriel appears to tell him of the impending birth of John. At the end, the disciples return to the temple with great joy, where they bless God (Luke 24:52–53). Much, of course, happens in between, but the joy of the disciples has familiar causes. The disciples, cast down and fearful after Jesus' death, have come to realize and experience him again, alive. They are filled with joy at the presence of their Lord, and more, they are filled with joy at this evidence from God that a new day is beginning. All nations will benefit from the witness and proclamation of the disciples, who themselves will be blessed with the presence of God's Holy Spirit. The presence of God, merciful and faithful, God now known in Jesus, whom the disciples worship (24:52), is cause for joy.

There is more in Luke's Gospel. Whenever one finds a word or phrase repeated frequently in a passage, as well as when a word or phrase frames a passage, the Gospel writer is drawing our attention to that literary clue. The parables of the lost sheep, coin, and son (or sons), clustered in Luke 15, share similar dynamics. These parables powerfully witness to the mercy and perseverance of God. They witness no less powerfully to an amazing joy, that is, God's own joy in finding and gathering in those who had been lost from God's people. In Luke 15:6, 7, 9, 10, and 32 we hear of joy and rejoicing. In case the reader doesn't make the leap from the rejoicing of a shepherd or a woman with ten coins, Luke makes it explicit that this is about joy in heaven over one sinner who returns to God (15:7, 10). Joy is not left in doubt in the last story. Verses 23, 24, and 29 are all about celebration, the expression of joy and gratitude. In verse 32, the chapter is summed up for the elder son and for every reader: "But we had to celebrate and rejoice, because this brother of yours was dead and has come to life; he was lost and has been found." Here joy in heaven matches and occasions human joy in the restoration of community, the restoration of relationship, and the right ordering of God's world brought about by God's powerful, merciful, and enduring yearning for all God's creatures.

More Gospel References to Joy

The Gospel writers know that joy can be dangerous. Luke knows of the kind of joy that can be heedless of God's command to love one's neighbor (Luke 12:19, for example). Joy can be easily expressed and short-lived, disappearing under the pressure of fear or doubt. The Gospel writers show us the crowd joyfully welcoming Jesus into Jerusalem. They remember how some welcomed the message of Jesus with joy, which was too shallow to be sustained (Matt. 13:20; Mark 4:16; Luke 8:13; 19:37). Nonetheless, joy is a wonderful sign of the presence of God and God's kingdom. It is an emotion humans know in part from their own relationships but much more fully in their connections with God and God's kingdom. John the Baptist uses such human joy to draw an analogy to his relationship with Jesus in John 3:29. There he compares himself to the friend of the bridegroom who rejoices at hearing his voice. Because John has heard the voice of Jesus, his own joy "has been fulfilled." In John 16:22 Jesus promises his disciples that pain will turn into joy itself, enduring joy, when they meet Jesus again after the crucifixion. He compares this joy to what a woman feels after a child is born. No matter the duress of labor, the joy of new life triumphs. So it will be in new life with Jesus.

Paul's Joy in Jesus, Messiah of God

Paul knew his Scriptures well. For him it was pure joy to experience and trust God's new era, God's triumph over death, and God's faithful love of all creation. A great place to catch Paul's thinking about joy is in his letter to the Philippians, written sometime between 50 and 60 CE. This letter is peppered with calls to rejoice, similar to those found in the Psalms. In fact, joy is a theme in this letter. In Philippians 1:4 joy appears as part of the thanksgiving, a section in which Paul often hints at the themes of the letter. He always prays with joy because of the mutual relationship possible in Christ between himself and the Philippians. It is the presence of God among them and the right relationships rooted in the love of God in Christ that bring Paul joy. Paul shares his joy with the people assembled to hear the letter.

The reader can just catch the liturgical rhythm, the back and forth between Paul and the congregation. I pray with joy, he says. No matter my circumstances, no matter the realities of human behavior, I rejoice when Christ is proclaimed. Christ is the gatherer, the creator of this community, the gift of God, and the model for the community's interactions. Paul finds joy in this work of

God and trusts that the Philippians also find such joy (Phil. 1:25). For their part, Paul encourages the Philippians to live in accord with the gospel and "complete" Paul's own joy (2:2). He calls upon this assembly of God's people in Christ Jesus to "rejoice in the Lord" (3:1; 4:4). Paul does not hide from difficulties even as he experiences joy. He finds joy and gladness in being "poured out"—used up, we might say—for the Philippians' faith (2:17). Even this joy is to be expressed mutually by Paul and the community. In this way Paul teaches what joy means for a Christian, namely, to be caught up in proclaiming the saving faithfulness of God in Christ. He creates a network of joy among the people and with God. Joy is central to the way Christians love and care for one another as children of God (2:29; 4:10).

Reflections

The Bible shows us joy among people at worship in prayer, dance, and song. It shows us joy at deep friendship, with passion for one another and for life, like the joy of a bride and bridegroom and their entire community. It shows us joy as trust in God's presence in good times and bad, both in the fullness of harvest and in the lamentations of a people who must imagine the joy of justice and peace ahead of them. It has shown us the joy of hopes fulfilled, of being remembered by God as all kinds of folks look forward to the birth of Jesus and then, later, to his second coming. We see Paul's expectation of joy as one of the fruits of God's holy presence in the Spirit and in Christ. Joy may well be understood as delight, actual or anticipated, in the fullness of God's blessings accompanied always by awareness of the One who provides.

Questions for Discussion

1. The Westminster Shorter Catechism states, "The chief end of man is to glorify God and enjoy Him forever." What does this sentence suggest about God? What do you enjoy? How do we enjoy God?

2. Does it seem to you that Christians have cultivated their capacity for enjoyment? How might we become Christian enjoyers, rather than people who enjoy what our culture teaches us to enjoy?

3. How might a Jew or a Christian distinguish between having fun and enjoying? What does it mean to enjoy?

4. Is there a way to be in joy during times of struggle, pain, or loss? Or do we simply confess, as did the writer of Lamentations, that joy has withered? How do you understand the difference between a confession of the loss of joy and Paul's insistence that we rejoice even as we are "poured out"?

Chapter Seven

Justice

> The LORD of hosts is exalted by justice, and the Holy God shows himself holy by righteousness.
>
> Isa. 5:16

E nglish-speaking North Americans enter a linguistic labyrinth when we consider the theme of justice in the Bible. Our English translations use two different word groups to translate the same Greek word. "Right" and its connected forms "righteous" and "righteousness" are used interchangeably with words from the Latin root, "just," "justice," "justify," and the like. Even though these two families of words translate the same Greek word into English, we have come to understand righteousness as different from justice and righteous as different from just. How are we to understand justice and its extraordinary importance in the biblical tradition? How can we grasp the way in which "justice" and "righteousness" (the same Greek word) bespeak our relationship with God?

To make matters even more confusing, our ideas in English about the difference in meaning between "justice" and "righteousness" mislead us about the interconnectedness of the Old and New Testaments. Gaining insight about this theme requires real attention to our biblical texts. This chapter is based on finding the Hebrew and

Greek words for justice in the original language of the texts and then trying to bring the connections, repetitions, and emphases of those texts to English readers. The upshot of this is that different translations have sometimes made different decisions of how the same Hebrew or Greek word is to be rendered in English.

Old Testament

There is a certain consistency about the concept of justice as the Old Testament witnesses to it. God created the earth and all its creatures, including those we humans think of as inanimate (the winds, for example). God, who alone fully comprehends the interconnections of all things and who alone fully imagines the future of all things, is alone the fully just one. God's role as judge and God's activity of judging are in the service of justice/righteousness. God's justice has everything to do with the restoration of *shalom*, the peace that passes understanding, the right-working of the universe.

In a wonderful passage from Genesis 18, Abraham argues with God about the destruction of Sodom. Their argument is precisely about justice and righteousness. God "thinks aloud" in 18:16–19. Because Abraham had been chosen to "keep the way of the LORD by doing righteousness and justice," God wants him to know about the coming punishment of Sodom and Gomorrah. This passage makes two points. First, God chooses Abraham to become a nation marked by the doing of justice in accord with God's will. Second, the doing of such justice and righteousness is not necessarily intuitive or instinctive: Abraham must be included as a kind of "justice-apprentice." God shares the plan to investigate the two sinful cities with Abraham (18:21), but Abraham hears more than God says.

In Genesis 18:23, he raises the question of God's destruction of the righteous with the wicked. Here the word for "righteous" is the same as the word for "just." "Will you indeed sweep away the righteous with the wicked?" Abraham asks. It is telling that the "wicked" in Genesis 18:23 are those who do not revere God. To be just (or righteous) is to revere God, the author of justice. It would be unjust to destroy those who live in accord with God's will. Abraham makes his main point in verse 25: "Shall not the Judge of all the earth do what is just?" The conversation continues, with Abraham growing increasingly nervous about pushing God. Yet God is the just one. In the end, God neither pursues injustice nor punishes Abraham.

Long before Abraham, God also grieved the sinfulness of humankind. In the story of Noah, God resolved to "blot out" humankind, given its sorry state of sinfulness. But Noah was a just man who lived in accord with God's will (Gen. 6:9–10). Because it would be unjust to destroy a righteous man, God saves Noah and his family, afterward making a covenant with Noah (6:18; 7:1). Recognizing the tragic reality that "the inclination of the human heart is evil from youth," God nevertheless promises never again to destroy every living creature. It would be unjust to destroy humankind for what it is, when there is not capacity to be—as a group—just. Justice demands that the weaknesses of the creature be included in expectations about behavior. Genesis 8:21–22 is God's profound commitment to justice that reaches beyond our imaginations.

Exodus

In Exodus God's justice is pitted against Pharaoh's failure to be just. God promises to exercise a great "judgment" against Pharaoh, a judgment necessitated by God's covenant with the Hebrews, who "groaned" in bondage, were unable properly to worship God while under Pharaoh's thumb, and no longer had confidence in God's commitment to them. Their spirits were broken; promises of judgment or justice were impossible for those broken by injustice to hear (Exod. 6:3–9). It was hard also for Pharaoh to hear the claims of justice on the part of his cheap labor force! God's clear determination to have justice for Israel wins the day: by God's justice/righteousness, Israel was led out of Egypt (Exod. 15:12).

Having been delivered, the Israelites are called to wrestle with justice as a group in covenant with that same God. This is the second great interest in justice that fills the Bible: justice within human communities of God's people. In Exodus 18, Jethro, father-in-law of Moses, spends time with Moses and the people in their encampment in the wilderness. Jethro knows about God's deliverance of the people from Egypt (18:1, 8–11). After acknowledging the just action and the power of God, Jethro watches Moses trying to mete out justice among the people. Moses' "judging" is the work of connecting the everyday lives of Israel with God's own "statutes and instructions" (v. 16), interpreting them to resolve disputes and questions of all sorts. This is the role of a human judge throughout the Bible. This story underlines the value and necessity of human work connecting God's commands with the lives of people. In fact, the work is so important that Moses must make provision for it to go forward when it becomes too much for one man alone. The will of God is teachable, says Jethro (v. 20). The qualifications for being a judge, making the connection between God and God's people to guide behavior in real life, are: fear of God, trustworthiness, impartiality, and ability to learn. Judging or providing justice has to do with helping human beings live in community as God wants. This work is necessary both because the community lives in covenant with God who has a specific character and because living is complex. Discerning justice in human community has never been a simple process. (Exodus 23 offers many examples of the radical nature of justice expected from God's people as well as some of the temptations that get in the way of justice.)

God's work of judging, justifying, and enacting justice carried out in the exodus is referred to frequently in the Old Testament. An explicit example of the connection of God's justice and human justice occurs in Leviticus 19:35–37, where "justice" ("honest" in NRSV) shows up four times. The honesty (justness) of transactions is directly tied to God, "who brought you out of the land of Egypt." See also Deuteronomy 1:16–18, where the story of Moses and Jethro is retold. An added feature of justice as understood in the exodus, which will also permeate the prophets' speeches, is that those who seek to discern and enact justice dare not be intimidated because it is God's judgment they bring.

Deuteronomy

Although God's people are called to lives of justice (righteousness), the biblical witness reminds us that it is not human justice that makes us appealing to God. In Deuteronomy 9:4–7 is a clear statement that the doing of justice may be a covenantal calling, but it is not a natural gift. Nor does God act graciously because we humans are righteous. "Righteousness" in these verses (NRSV) comes from the same root words as the "justice" that we have already seen in Genesis, Exodus, and Leviticus. Consider the powerful command in Deuteronomy 16:18–20, ending with "Justice, and only justice, you shall pursue, so that you may live and occupy the land that the LORD your God is giving you." This justice must not be mistaken for some disinterested following of a code. If that's all there were to justice, it would be simple. But justice involves bringing a code to life and rendering decisions for the people. It also requires us to be alert to our own blind spots.

"O mortal . . . do justice"

The prophets do not let us forget this calling. This watchword from Micah 6:8 should be memorized: "[God] has told you, O mortal, what is good; and what does the LORD require of you but to do justice, and to love kindness, and to walk humbly with your God?" God's people receive a vocation that begins with doing justice. Even as human vocation is clear, so also is the prophetic naming and decrying of human injustice. Injustice brings down terrible consequences, whether on Israel or on the nations. Doing justice/righteousness brings life. According to Ezekiel 18, injustice/unrighteousness can kill the practitioner. In this chapter Israel is imagined as seeking justice against God. The charge? "The way of the Lord is unfair" (Ezek. 18:25). Such a charge would be a sure sign that Israel does not know God. Indeed, says God in response to such a charge, "I have no pleasure in the death of anyone. . . . Turn, then, and live." The turn needed is away from injustice and toward righteousness/justice, God's will for the world.

The Poetics of Justice

Isaiah. As we prepare to move into the New Testament, let us look at just a few of the ways justice emerges as thematic in the Psalms and Isaiah, two books very different from one another yet beloved of early Christian writers. Isaiah's interest in justice permeates the entire book, from chapter 1 through chapter 66. Isaiah describes the failures of the people to be faithful to God. They have strayed from worship of God. They have abandoned justice with one another, particularly the oppressed. The failure to live justly corrupts Israel in the eyes of God, undermines all claims to faithfulness, and brings about terrible consequences for the people themselves. "Cease to do evil, learn to do good," says God through the prophet. The doing of good is further defined: "Seek justice, rescue the oppressed, defend the orphan, plead for the widow"(Isa. 1:16–17). Faithfulness to God is impossible without justice. The connection between being the vineyard of God and justice shows up in poetic form in Isaiah 5:7, 16, the latter a key verse: "The LORD of hosts is exalted by justice, and the Holy God shows himself holy by righteousness" (compare 30:18; 33:22). It is God's justice, God's righteousness, that undergirds, underlines, and demands human justice. Even if all humanity or the universe itself were to be unjust or untrue to promises, the Lord remains the one who can be trusted. If you hear echoes of Romans 8:31–39 here, you are right on.

In fact, it is the very calling of Israel to "bring forth justice to the nations" (Isa. 42:1). This verse and indeed the entire chapter came to be understood by Christians as describing the work of Jesus. Jesus, for believers, became the servant who carried God's spirit, in order to bring justice to all the earth. Jesus was God's way of creating a covenant with all people, the very nations who had persecuted Israel (42:5–6). In its original voice, the passage witnesses to the work of a people to spread God's spirit of justice. It is the very justice/righteousness of God *not* to abandon all that God had created but to find a way to redeem all creation. In Isaiah 59:16–20 it is God who must take up the cause of justice when there is no one else to do so. The promise of redemption of those who have been in mourning re-creates them as "oaks of righteousness" (61:3). God will make fruitful God's garden or vineyard, the earth, by causing "righteousness and praise to spring up" (61:11). Here the integral, almost organic quality of justice/righteousness is clear. When the earth is truly the Lord's in every way, it flowers in justice and joy.

Psalms. For early Christians Jesus' resurrection began to usher in God's ultimately redeemed cosmos as Isaiah understood it. Israel's beloved psalms also express this profound hope in God's justice. The powerful description of God's salvation, surely "at hand" (Ps. 85:9), envisions the inseparable realities of God, steadfast love and faithfulness, righteousness and peace. Earth will be enveloped in faithfulness and righteousness, from ground and sky. The word for "righteousness/justice" occurs three times in three verses: it is the hallmark of God's presence, God's will done, and a source of joy for God's people (Ps. 85:6, 10–13).

Although Psalm 119 is not always well appreciated by Christians, in this psalm, as nowhere else, one can see the connection of delight, decrees, and divine justice. The word for "decree" in the Greek Old Testament is simply a noun made from the word for "just." Decrees of God are about and embody justice. Such decrees or precepts (e.g., Ps. 119:2, 4, 7, 8, 12, 16, and so on) are a source of joy because they are godly. Deeply understanding them brings one closer to a delight in relationship to God (see, for instance, vv. 30, 32, 35). These signs of justice are a joy worthy of meditation because they are signs of God's own self. There is no cold law code here that God's people struggle grudgingly to keep. Instead, there is that sense of organic connection that we saw in Isaiah, a way in which life in God's vineyard is fruitful, filled with all that allows God's creatures of every sort to live in peace and in joy—in a word, justly.

New Testament

The authors of the early Christian Greek writings were shaped not only by Jewish Scripture but also by the very Greek world in which they lived. After the time of Alexander the Great, in the third century BCE, Greek culture spread along the Mediterranean coast. Greek was the language of commerce, governance, and learning. Among the Greeks, justice was as important as it was among the Jews, being understood as one of the four cardinal virtues to which humankind ought aspire. Justice was, therefore, considered throughout the ancient world as a great good; Greek thought supported scriptural truth. But Scripture tied justice closely to God as the ultimately just judge whose very commands were justice itself. Christians who claimed to belong to God without following scriptural precepts had to come to some understanding of how they might be just followers of a just God. It is no accident that Matthew, Luke-Acts, and Romans have the highest number of references to the "justice" word group. Matthew has twenty-two, Luke-Acts thirty-one, and Romans fifty-five. Even a short letter like Galatians, where Paul is struggling with how one might delight in God and yet not keep all God's ordinances (controverting Ps. 119), has eleven uses of these words.

Paul

Romans 3 is a tightly written, complex unit of Paul's thought, one of whose central themes is justice/righteousness and its opposite. Fundamentally, Paul continues to think within the biblical tradition that justice/righteousness means life for humans (see Rom. 8:10). As we have seen, justice/righteousness is defined—perhaps "learned" is a better word—in relationship with God, the source of all justice/righteousness, rather than in relationship to an abstract moral code. In his letter to the Romans, Paul introduces his central idea early in the letter. Romans 1:16–17 is about the justice/righteousness of God, that quality of God that, Paul claims, has been revealed through the gospel. We must imagine that Paul knows his Scripture (our Old Testament) very well indeed. He himself has been a person of faith, trusting that God is a trustworthy keeper of covenantal promises. As the prophets before him had observed, the conditions in which Israel finds itself (governed by non-Israelites, scattered, and far from prosperous) are not what God promised. Surely it must be that Israel has continued to endure the consequences of its own failure to abide justly in covenant with God. When God raised Jesus from death, Paul and other followers of Christ believed that God's justice, mercy, and faithfulness were renewed on earth. Furthermore, God's Spirit appeared among Jews and Gentiles. Trusting in God who raised Jesus, therefore, was a just/righteous response for all people.

Justice/righteousness in covenant relationship with the God who defines justice/righteousness had become available to humans in Christ Jesus. God's justice/righteousness made clear in the story of Jesus (the gospel) is God's redemption of creation as promised to Noah, Abraham, David, and, through them, to humankind as a whole. Human justice/righteousness becomes connected to the relationship with and experience of God in Jesus the Messiah. Even though this may sound like a topic other than that of "justice," we are dealing here with one family of words in Greek, not two different families as English would suggest. The just treatment of others, as has always been a part of covenant relationship with God, continues. We hear of it in the New Testament as loving the neighbor as oneself, as caring for the sister or brother for whom Christ died (Rom. 14–15).

In Romans 15:9–12, Paul quotes several passages of Scripture to make the point that God had always intended to include Gentiles among God's people. Justice would have it so. With Jesus' resurrection, a new day had begun. Justice was no longer impossible for humans but made possible through God's empowering Spirit. Human justice (or righteousness) now is to be like God's justice, reaching out also to the unjust ("sinners" in Rom. 5) and gathering them in for the upbuilding of God's people. Justice includes mercy; indeed, mercy helps to define justice. Again, justice is no cold code by which rewards and punishments are meted out. Instead, justice is that quality of God and humans where the just/right thing is done for the well-being of God's creatures in community. "Community," waiting and longing for the freedom of a just relationship with God, includes all that is (Rom. 8:19–23).

The Gospels

In the writings of Luke and Matthew, justice/righteousness is significant for the rich variety of senses brought forward from the Old Testament, from Jesus, and from the Greco-Roman world.

Luke offers a measure of the importance and shades of difference in understanding justice/righteousness. He begins his Gospel in an almost palpably Jewish temple scene in which Zechariah and Elizabeth, parents of John the Baptist, are both described as just/righteous before God (Luke 1:6). Their justice/righteousness is in regard to life in accord with God's covenantal commands. Near the end of the Gospel (Luke 23:47), a centurion proclaims that Jesus truly was righteous/just—or, as in many translations, innocent (see also Matt. 27:4, 19, 24). The centurion, a Roman military man, was not thinking about Jesus and Jewish law. Luke has swept us along from right relationship with God in Israel to a cosmic conviction of justice/"righteousness" uttered by a representative of the Roman Empire. The centurion is correct. Jesus is identified as "the Holy and Righteous One" (Acts 3:14) and "the Righteous One" (Acts 7:52). Such a characterization argues on the basis of Jesus' resurrection, that his death on the cross was not a sign of his failure to be faithful to God—indeed, just the opposite. To claim that Jesus is the Righteous One is to put forward the understanding of justice/righteousness as doing God's will in the world and seeking right relationship and human thriving, even if one's interpretation of scriptural commands is at odds with the tradition.

A similar sense of justice and righteousness animates Matthew's depictions of the final judgment. When God comes finally to judge the world and restore creation to rightness, the basis for judgment of humankind will be righteous/just deeds. In Matthew 25:31–46, the parable of the sheep and the goats, the just/righteous ones (25:37–39) are surprised, even mystified by their inclusion among those who served Jesus. But their service is a mark of their justice/righteousness. God's justice and life in accord with it seeks out and includes those in need. Justice is about the sharing of all that is required for life. The Gospel writers claim that Jesus, crucified as seditious and mocked as a blasphemer, was in fact just. Luke's parable of the Pharisee and the tax collector shares the conviction that the one who appears to be just by all the external signs may well be fooling everyone, himself included. The one who turns to God always, seeking God's will and mercy humbly, is the one in right relationship with God and, presumably, humans as well.

Reflections

The Bible summons us to be just/righteous in regard to God's covenant commands. This call shaped the words of the prophets, the Psalms, Wisdom writings, and Jewish belief. God's commands were in service of God's commitment to the just/right interworkings of creation, that all might be fed and live (see Ps. 104). One who served this justice was just. One who did not went to live among the goats or, as Luke suggests in 13:27 (where the NRSV "evildoers" is a translation of "unjust"), to weeping and gnashing of teeth outside of God's banquet. An excellent illustration of this is the parable of the rich man and Lazarus (Luke 16:19–31; cf. Matt. 25:31–46). Here a well fed, clothed, and housed rich man treats wretchedly a poor man at his gate and lands in "hell," while the poor man goes to "heaven." It is striking in this parable that Father Abraham reminds the rich man that "Moses and the prophets" make amply clear God's call for justice, even for the most voiceless of God's creatures. Jesus tells the parable as a way to interpret his calling and that of his disciples. God still calls for justice/righteousness, a life lived in merciful outreach for the sake of a suffering world.

Questions for Discussion

1. How does it change the meaning for you if we translate all the occurrences of "righteousness" in the NRSV translation of Deuteronomy 9:4–7 as "justice"? What if we translate similar occurrences in Romans 1 this way?
2. How does "think globally, act locally" capture the idea of justice in the Bible? What might be missed by such a formulation?
3. Life often looks unfair. What does that suggest about God? About us?

Chapter Eight

Love

Beloved, let us love one another, because love is from
God.

1 John 4:7

The English word "love" translates a number of different
Greek and Hebrew words from the Old and New Testaments. While much has been written about these terms, the
report of significant differences has been exaggerated. Different
writers sometimes use one term more than another. But in general, "love" translates words that describe God's deep attachment
to Israel and God's larger creation, creation's deep attachment to
God, and the core relationship among humans, one neighbor to
another. As we will see, love refers to emotion and also to behavior. One loves in a very active way, as actively as the God who first
loved us, whether Israel or the body of Christ.

In the Bible those who seek God always wrestle with what
God's love means for them and for the world around them. The
New Testament writers had to wrestle as well with how God
"loved" the son who died on the cross. Vulnerability is one characteristic of love that emerges strongly. The one who loves is vulnerable to those who are beloved. God is vulnerable to pain,
frustration, sorrow, and joy at the hands of those whom God has
chosen to love. Jesus shows us that vulnerability clearly. His res-

urrection shows us that God's power to continue loving will not be destroyed by vulnerability, but deepened.

Old Testament

In the Old Testament, love—indeed, steadfast love—is central to who God is. It is a vital part of God's character. A relationship of love, gratuitously given and forever faithful, determines God's relationship to creation and most especially to Israel. Love is central also to God's people: Israel is called to abide in love of God and live out this same relationship with humans.

God's Love Is Foundational for Israel

In Exodus 20:1–6, God clearly identifies God's self to Moses before giving him what Christians call the Ten Commandments. God's commands rest on a foundation of love and faithfulness from God toward humankind. "I am the LORD your God, who brought you out of the land of Egypt, out of the house of slavery," God says. This rescue was an act of love first to the generation who left Egypt, then to their descendents forever. In Exodus 20:6 (see also Deut. 5:10), God proclaims that steadfast love characterizes his relationship with the faithful. In Deuteronomy 4:37 God's love and God's delivery from Egypt are explicitly connected. It is God's character to love, and God's actions reveal or, better, constitute that love.

Deuteronomy explores God's love as God's relationship of choice with Israel. In fact, God's rescue of Israel from Egypt is connected to God's love again in Deuteronomy 7:8. In the preceding verse, the people are reminded of an identifying quality of God's love—that it is simply given, never fully deserved or understandable according to human categories: "It was not because you were more numerous than any other people that the LORD set his heart on you and chose you—for you were the fewest of all peoples." How to understand a God who makes such choices? There is no understanding. There is only the acceptance of the relationship of love with its consequences. Love continues to be thematic in Deuteronomy 10. Moses reviews the people's history with God, remembering with them how they had gotten from Egypt almost to the promised land itself. The implied question of Israel's obligation for this care is voiced in 10:12: "What does the LORD your God require of you?" The obligation is, "Only to fear the LORD your God, to walk in all his ways, to love him, to serve the LORD your God with all your heart and with all your soul." Some ways in which Israel can do these things follow directly in the text. Love is active. All four of the requirements Moses describes stand in apposition to one another: "fear," "walk in all his ways," "love," and "serve" all describe the same relationship, the same way of being God's people. We should hear well what is said here, for it will resurface in the Gospels.

The miracle of God's love undergirds the call to the people. In 10:15 Israel is once again reminded of the astounding reality that the creator of all chose them. Love unearned and freely given connects the people to God. God's commandments are given in love for the people's "well-being" (10:13). How important it is that Moses adds just a few verses later that God also cares for the needy and "loves the strangers" (10:18). Even though God has loved and chosen Israel, Israel is not the limit of God's love. No, God loves strangers and provides for them. Furthermore, Israel as God's own people is also called to love the stranger (10:19). Israel is called to provide for the stranger as God once provided for Israel.

Finally, near the end of Deuteronomy, Moses again reminds the people that they have choices to make about their relationship with God. To love God (see 30:15, 20) is to serve God, walk in God's ways, keep God's commandments, and be blessed. The love of God is life itself to Israel. Lest we hear this as an impossible demand from God, let us hear the promise of God in Deuteronomy 30:6: At a time when Israel seems as lost as can be, at a time when the covenant with God seems irremediably broken and perhaps forgotten by God, the people who turn to God will be circumcised of heart, both they and their children, with the purpose of enabling them to "love the LORD your God with all your heart and with all your soul, in order that you may live." God will make it possible for those who turn to him or call upon his name to love him. Even that love which is commanded of humans does not come from human power alone: God enables the relationship God seeks, a relationship of active love.

Indeed, it is the watchword of Israel, the sacred confession that Jews till this day seek to have on their lips in life and at the moment of death that proclaims this relationship: "Hear, O Israel: The LORD is our God, the LORD alone. You shall love the LORD your God with all your heart, and with all your soul, and with all your might" (6:4–5). This is the first and greatest commandment also according to Jesus (see Matt. 22:36–38; Mark 12:29–30; Luke 10:25–28). It is not the only great commandment, however, and the second also has to do with love.

Love of God and Love of Neighbor

"Love" is a very active word. God loves by faithfully choosing, rescuing, calling, empowering, commanding, creating, and pro-tecting, to name just a few actions. Humans love by obeying, fol-lowing, confessing God alone as God, and worshiping, also to name just a few actions. As we have seen, however, humans are called to actions that are like those of God. They are called to love each other and even to love the stranger by providing food, drink, and safety. Human love is shown at least by doing justice, even more by loving mercy (see Mic. 6:8). It is also shown by loyalty and steadfastness in relationship and care. Naomi is reminded in the story of Ruth that her daughter-in-law loves her and is more to her "than seven sons" (Ruth 4:15).

Steadfast loyalty and human affection are abundantly witnessed to in the Bible, as are their opposites. The long saga of David, shepherd boy become king deeply beloved by God, is full of such examples. Saul's deceitful love that seeks to entrap David appears in 1 Samuel 18:22. Saul's son Jonathan loves David and saves his life only two chapters later (1 Sam. 20:17). David's terrible love for Bathsheba leads him to sacrifice one of his captains to have her as his wife (2 Sam.11–12). The cruelty of human love and the con-fusion of lust and love are made harshly clear in the story of

Amnon and Tamar, children of David (2 Sam. 13:4, 15). But the misuse of love between humans does not lead only to suspicion of love's value and power. The Song of Solomon reminds us of love's joy between a man and a woman. There are innumerable similes in which God's relationship to Israel is likened to that of a bridegroom for a bride. Children are beloved. Friendships exist. What makes these human loves strong and good is understanding them as created by God for our well-being.

When Tamar stands in fear before Amnon, unprotected in the face of his lust for her, she insists, "No, my brother, do not force me; for such a thing is not done in Israel; do not do anything so vile!" Israel, in a right relationship of love of God that is characterized by keeping God's commandments so that all may live, would not condone human love run amok. As ever, the Bible shows us some sad realities about human relationships while at the same time making clear what God's command is for us. In Leviticus 19:17–18 Moses speaks for God and announces, "You shall not hate in your heart anyone of your kin; you shall reprove your neighbor. . . . You shall not take vengeance or bear a grudge against any of your people, but you shall love your neighbor as yourself: I am the LORD." The command to love one's neighbor— and this command extends both to one's neighbor within Israel and to others (see Lev. 19:33–34)—is to be characteristic of God's people, even as God has loved them when they were still unworthy. We will also hear this command in the New Testament, joined to that of loving God. These two loves go hand in hand. They cannot be separated.

The Prophets Witness to God's Call for Loving Justice

Law and prophets make clear that any claim to love God while treating the neighbor unjustly is a claim unfounded. God will not accept human love as such if those who profess such love harm others. Actions speak very loudly of love—or not. God's actions speak of the expansiveness of God's love as well as its steadfastness. Perhaps it is always a quality of human beings that we seek to circumscribe and manage God's love as best we can. But the

Bible reminds us ever and again that our imagination of God's love in no way comes close to accuracy. The Bible stretches and challenges our imagination in Old Testament and New. Isaiah 56 is a wonderful reminder of our inability to set a limit on God's love. In this hope-filled pasage, readers have already heard that the very mountains and hills will burst into song and applause from joy in God's return (55:12–13). It will be such a time of deliverance and salvation from enemies and oppression that all will be invited to share in the blessings. Eunuchs and foreigners who had had no place in God's temple hold a place in God's heart and among God's people. No one remains distant; no one who "loves the name of the LORD" and serves the Lord will be excluded from joy and acceptance: "Thus says the Lord GOD, who gathers the outcasts of Israel, I will gather others to them besides those already gathered" (56:8). We do not know who these others might be. Many of the Jews in the time of Jesus believed that God was gathering in Gentiles by the power of the Holy Spirit. How unpredictably this God works to call and bless those who love God, whether God's people recognize them or not! This is the love of the Creator for those he has made. This is the love that yearns for all to be gathered into a covenant that begins with the words, "I am the Lord your God." This is the vulnerable love that comes to us in Jesus of Nazareth and does not stop loving us even when we crucify love itself.

New Testament

God's Commands at the Heart of the Gospels

Jesus' two central commands were taken directly from his Scripture, our Old Testament. These two commands gather up and summarize the two ways in which God invites us to be in relationship with God and one another: Love God with all your heart and soul (Deut. 10:12) and "love your neighbor as yourself" (Lev. 19:18). The Gospel writers Matthew, Mark, and Luke showcase these words of Jesus. In Luke 10:27, the commands are put into the mouth of the Bible scholar who is asking what he must do "to inherit eternal life." Jesus says, "You've got it right," when the scholar (called "lawyer" in many translations) cites these two love commands as all that God requires. The discussion is pushed to a second level as the man tries to figure out to whom he owes love. Whom must I love? This is not a silly question, for love involves commitments that are far from easy to keep. In Luke's Gospel Jesus expects that people both understand that God calls on us to love each other *and* that we can do it (see, for example, the parable of the rich man and Lazarus in Luke 16:19–31).

In Matthew 22:37 Jesus himself quotes the two commands. Matthew's Gospel places these commands a bit later in Jesus' ministry and in the context of hostile questioning. In Matthew 22:15 we hear that the Pharisees "plotted to entrap him in what he said." This is followed by a series of questions from different groups. The Pharisees are the last group to question Jesus. Again a Bible scholar ("lawyer") asks him a question "to test him": "Teacher, which commandment in the law is the greatest?" Jesus answers first with reference to love of God from Deuteronomy and second with love of neighbor from Leviticus. He concludes, "on these two commandments hang all the law and the prophets" (22:34–40). This is a defining statement about how this early movement of believers in Jesus as Messiah was to shape itself in regard to Scripture.

Mark 12:28–34 seems to be the earlier version of Matthew's narrative. As in Matthew's Gospel, this summary too is close to the end of the Gospel in a scene where various subgroups among the Jews try to trap Jesus in his own speech (Mark 12:13). A scribe poses the question as part of an ongoing debate among Jesus and the Sadducees about interpreting Scripture. Teachers in Israel (those who sought to interpret their lives in light of the Scripture) learned by arguing point-counterpoint, by posing questions and considering responses. In fact, as Mark has it, the scribe asks Jesus which commandment is "first of all" because the scribe appreciated Jesus' answers to an earlier question (Mark 12:28). Jesus answers with the Shema, the age-old cry of Israel from Deuteronomy 6:4, and follows up with Leviticus. The scribe is excited by

Jesus' response. In this story, he agrees that Jesus is right and extends Jesus' reply to say that such love is more important than all the commands about sacrifice and offering. The connection between love of neighbor and love of God had long been made by God's prophets (see Amos 5, where all worship, including offerings and sacrifices, is despised if folk are mistreating their neighbors). Jesus connects this love intimately to the kingdom of God (Mark 12:34).

Love of God and One Another in Paul's Letters

Writing even earlier than the Gospel writers, Paul insists that "love your neighbor as yourself" is the proper summary of all the commands of the law (Rom. 13:9; Gal. 5:14). He adds that love "does no wrong to a neighbor," and it is in this doing no wrong that it fulfills the law (Rom. 13:10). In fact, in Romans 12 Paul writes about the life to which Christ's followers are called and for which they are empowered by the Holy Spirit. Love is of high importance. Romans 12:9–21 might be thought of as an extended discussion of love: "Let love be genuine; . . . love one another with mutual affection; outdo one another in showing honor" (vv. 9–10). Love is actively engaged in supporting, encouraging, and serving others. The language in Galatians is about bearing "one another's burdens" as a way to fulfill the "law of Christ," that is, the law of love (Gal. 6:2). This ability to love is a gift of the Spirit as well as a command. It is in fact the first-mentioned gift of the Spirit in Galatians 5:22 (see also 1 Thess. 3:12–13; 4:9–10). To deepen your idea of "love" in the hierarchical Mediterranean culture, simply read the descriptions of works of the flesh (the ways of the world) as love's opposites in Galatians 5:19–21.

Paul also left us the Bible's best-known testimony to love in 1 Corinthians 13. Love is highlighted here more clearly and more poetically than anywhere else. Although this passage is often read at weddings, the love evoked is not about romance but about the relations within a community. Love is the most necessary gift and profound gift of God because love alone, giving of self in care of the other, prevails in the face of all that we humans can be. Love is for everyone and is called forth from everyone. No one is too haughty, too low, too proud, too sure, too doubtful to love God and neighbor. It is this love that never ends; love is the essence of eternal life in God.

God's Self-Giving Love in John

All this love—that of God, that of neighbor—in both Old Testament and New is modeled, given, and strengthened by God's overwhelming love for all creation. John's Gospel puts this love before us in John 3:16, characterizing God by the very nature of God's love. We often hear the "so" in "For God so loved the world" as "so much." It is better understood as "in this way": "God loved the world in this way." The "way" is that of nonmutual self-giving. God loved the world in this way, that God gave God's own son with the purpose that everyone who believes in him may not perish but have eternal life. This is a God who does not seek to judge or condemn, both opposites of love. Rather, God loves by relinquishing power, privilege, ease, and all that might be God's for the sake of a people's living relationship with God. It is this love that Jesus enacts and calls upon his disciples also to enact with one another (John 13:34). We have seen that this commandment is not entirely "new," though its reach is now into peoples formerly not seen as beloved of God. The focus of John's writing is to keep this love in the forefront of Christian imagination. The entirety of 1 John speaks of love over and over again: "Little children, let us love, not in word or speech, but in truth and action" (1 John 3:18). This love of one another is as Jesus commanded (3:23), as the Spirit grants, and is a taste of full life in God's kingdom (4:7).

Reflections

God's love is a model for earthly loves, not the other way around. God's heart was set first on Israel, then through Israel's own traditions and peoples, and through Jesus on all people. God's presence, God's torah, God's Holy Spirit, God's son teach, model, and empower human love. Human love, therefore, is shaped by such commitment to the well-being of another that it will set aside self-interest for the sake of the other. This dynamic permeates our biblical understanding of whom we are called to serve and whom we are called to be in this cosmos.

Questions for Discussion

1. The word "love" means many things to different people. Even when we agree that we should love our neighbor, child, parents, or country, we have different ideas about what is the best way to love. What is your fundamental understanding of love? Can you come up with a "bottom line" definition of love about which you think Christians might be able to agree?

2. From your perspective, what makes love difficult? Why don't we just "all get along"?

3. Law and prophets make clear that any claim to love God while treating the neighbor unjustly is a claim unfounded. God will not accept human love as such, if those who profess such love harm others. What might such prophets single out among us today as signs of our not loving?

4. Contrast John 3:16 and 3:19. How do you understand these two "loves"? (John 12:43 offers some help.) How would you talk about darkness in the contemporary world? What makes darkness attractive and light less so? Can the church be of any use in clarifying the limitations of a life lived in darkness?

Chapter Nine

Peace

Righteousness and peace will kiss each other.
Ps. 85:10

"Think globally, act locally" is a slogan that encapsulates many biblical themes. We are called by Scripture to stretch our limited imagination to its utmost, trying to grasp the global, or better, cosmic, reign of God. We are equally called, however, to live as best we can in accord with this vision. Justice calls for continuing revisioning, as we learn more and more from one another as God's beloved creatures. The process of trying to live in accord with our best understanding of and trust in God is discipleship. Peace, biblically speaking, is the condition of human and nonhuman communities living justly with one another on this dear earth, according to God's deepest desires and creativity. In this section we will see how peace is both global and local. The most common words for "peace," *shalom* in Hebrew and *eirene* in Greek, describe not being at war, the ground for a full reign of peace. Peace, however, goes much deeper than cessation of violent hostilities. That larger vision of peace is also described frequently. The word "peace" is so basic to our true hope for life that it is a greeting shared throughout the Bible, Old Testament and New, among those who wish one another life in the best possible world.

88

Old Testament

There are over three hundred uses of the word "peace" in the Old Testament, most of them concerned with conditions of peace between peoples or with greetings. The very absence of peace creates a deep appreciation of it. All the blessings God promises require a field of peace in order to grow and thrive. It is abundantly clear in the Bible (and in our own time) that peace is at the same time actively to be sought and received as a blessing of God. Peace as a blessing becomes part of the vision of what God will grant in that glorious future when God's way is fully realized.

Peace is part of God's covenant with Israel in Leviticus 26:6. God is represented as speaking through Moses, making clear commands, claims, and promises that shape God's relationship to Israel. Most important is the two-part refrain, "I am the LORD your God" (Lev. 26:13) and "you shall be my people" (26:12). God promises that faithful covenant keeping by Israel will result in abundance of food and a secure life: "I will grant peace in the land, and you shall lie down, and no one shall make you afraid" (26:6). Neither the danger of wild animals nor of human warfare will shake the people. Indeed, God will walk among them (26:12), look with favor upon them, and maintain the covenant. Here is a full vision of peace, part of which is the absence of danger or want, and part of which is the presence of God.

A story from the life of Isaac, son of Abraham, connects the presence of God, the creation of abundance, and the absence of warfare (Gen. 26). In this story Isaac follows the command of God to settle in Gerar among strangers. When he prospers more and more in that land, King Abimelech sends him and his household away because Isaac has become "too powerful" (v. 16). The command to go, Isaac's departure, and his subsequent settlement in a place where a new uncontested well had been dug proceed without violent confrontation. Isaac's success in finding water and relocating impresses Abimelech as much as his earlier agricultural prosperity had. The king comes to Isaac, saying, "We see plainly that the LORD has been with you; so we say, let there be an oath between you and us, and let us make a covenant with you so that you will do us no harm, just as we have not touched you and have done to you nothing but good and have sent you away in peace. You are now the blessed of the LORD" (vv. 28–29). In this story, Isaac's obedience to God results in a visible, tangible blessedness and peace with powerful neighbors.

Another facet of the biblical vision of peace is that right application of God's law also creates peace, as seen in the story of Moses and Jethro (Exod. 18:23). Israel, no matter how numerous and intractable its problems and questions might be, could receive justice, which would result in peace. Sirach 1:18 catches this sensibility: "The fear of the Lord is the crown of wisdom, making peace and perfect health to flourish." Peace and perfect health did not, however, flourish during most of Israel's history. This reality is laid to human behavior. It is the basis for much biblical prayer (Psalms) and for the prophets' words of condemnation or hope.

Prophets Speak of Peace to Come

Peace becomes a sign of life lived in accord with God, even if this kind of life is a hope for a future that seems far away. In Micah 5:2–5, for example, the longed-for peace is promised when someone unnamed comes from "one of the little clans" to "feed his flock in the strength of the LORD." This one will be a great ruler over all the earth, thus ensuring peace.* Again security is highlighted, reminding us how fragile any sense of safety must have been. The one to come "shall be the one of peace." A similar passage, Zechariah 8:10–19, promises peace, including safety from enemies and the doing of justice that "makes for peace."

The kind of prophecy in Micah shows up elsewhere. Isaiah promises, in words that Handel has made famous, that a son will be given who will be called "Mighty God . . . Prince of Peace" and who will inaugurate a reign of endless peace, upheld with justice and righteousness. Isaiah predicts the coming of a great king in

---

*Centuries later these words were applied to Jesus in Matt. 2:6 and perhaps John 7:40–43.

Israel who will fulfill God's covenant made with David (Isa. 9:6–7). Isaiah 32 recounts a great longing for peace, a longing as alive among us as it was thousands of years ago, and speaks of the transformation of humankind that will make it possible. In Isaiah 32:2–5, where eyes and ears previously closed will be open and minds reshaped, it is clear that peace and justice require great change in human behavior. There will be a just ruler, a "spirit from on high [will be] poured out on us," "justice will dwell in the wilderness," and the effect will be peace (32:15–17).

In parallel with "peace," and explaining it, are two words: "quietness" and "trust." Isaiah's statement (32:17) is a declaration of hope and trust; the time for peace has not yet arrived. The reiteration of the theme of promised peace occurs in Jeremiah 33:5–9. Human wickedness has brought a consequential destruction. Even though the wickedness has not ended, God promises freedom from guilt, recovery of peace and abundance, and awareness of God as the author of their blessing. For a summary of this promise, Jeremiah 33:14–16 is well-suited, although the word "peace" does not appear. In the future, God promises, because God will keep the covenants made so long ago; justice and righteousness will prevail throughout Israel. This future peace will see a righteous one on David's throne, and a true priesthood. The words "saved" and "safety" are used to describe Israel's condition of peace, which will happen "in those days."

As the Bible is determined to warn us, this peace is neither simple to discern nor bring about. Peace is the result of living justly or righteously. It is life lived in accord with God's arrangement of the world. When humankind lives unjustly, deceives or cheats, is driven by greed or by despair in God's presence and power, there is no peace. Israel's prophets warn against false prophets who declare peace when there is none. Their warnings remind people that peace will not take up residence unless they are living justly. In addition, prophets warn that God is not fooled by pretense of devotion. Ezekiel 13 is but one example of the dangers of prophets who lie about God's determined opposition to evildoing in order to bring false comfort. A prophet must neither lie nor prophesy apart from God's spirit (see especially vv. 1–2, 8, 10, 16). Truth-telling and true peace go together. "Whitewashing" or "glossing over" truth to feign peace while malfeasance continues is bound to fail. A people's designated leaders, rulers, and seers may all fail to be truthful. Ezekiel 34 speaks famously against Israel's plundering rulers who destroy the peace by failing the people. God will judge them and transform the situation: "I will save my flock" (v. 22). God's saving is expressed once again by the phrase "covenant of peace" (v. 25) within which all live securely and in abundance. Shame, hunger, thirst, slavery, and fear are destroyed. God is present and there is peace (vv. 25–31). See also Micah 3:5 and Jeremiah 4:10; 6:14; 8:11, 15; and 14:13–19 for naming the dangers of deceit in proclaiming peace.

The Psalms: Yearning for Peace

Seeking peace is a painful subject in our own time. What happened to human dreams and God's promise of peace? What is the work of a peacemaker? We will see these questions arise again in the New Testament, but first we must at least catch a glimpse of the deep desire for peace in the Psalms. The psalmist knows of and prays not to be numbered among prophets who speak of peace but work woe (Ps. 28:3). The prayer is that God will bless God's people with peace (29:11), yet an equally ardent prayer is that God's covenant people will actively seek peace. There is no contradiction. Peace, like justice, is characteristic of and a gift of God. At the same time, God's people are called to be just and seek peace. Psalm 34:14 simply states, "Depart from evil, and do good; seek peace, and pursue it." Psalm 37 enjoins hearers not to worry about, let alone envy, evildoers who seem to prosper, but to trust in the Lord, do good, wait patiently, and refrain from anger. The rewards for such behavior include security (37:3) and abundant peace (37:11). Finally, Psalm 72 is a prayer for blessing a king and brings together so beautifully justice, righteousness, abundance of food, and peace. Such a king has not yet come to reign fully among God's people, but the prayer for his coming signals our hope and the hope of the New Testament writers: "In his days may righteousness flourish and peace abound, until the moon is no more" (72:7).

New Testament

Jesus, Prince of Peace

Hope for peace persisted into Jesus' day both because and in spite of the fact that the world was so often embroiled in war or the threats and preparations for it. Those who believed that Jesus was God's Messiah applied scriptural prophecies of peace to him. Luke in particular makes this connection. Zechariah ends his prophetic song, sung under the power of the Holy Spirit, by quoting Isaiah 9:2, where God promises to "guide our feet into the way of peace." This guiding is exactly what God is up to in the work of John and, even more so, of Jesus. Shepherds hear a whole choir of angels herald Jesus' birth as the coming of peace among those whom God favors (Luke 2:14). It's a sea change for sure. When Simeon, in the Spirit's power, sees the newborn Jesus, he also sees God's promised "salvation," a sign of God's faithfulness that allows him to die "in peace" (2:29). Remembering all those wonderful prophecies of peace, especially to those who had been so desperately oppressed, we can hear God coming to set things right at last. No wonder joy, right along with peace, is such a hallmark of Luke's Gospel.

In Acts 10:36, Peter succinctly informs the Roman centurion Cornelius what God has been doing in Jesus. To all of Israel, God was "preaching peace by Jesus Christ." This peace, it turns out, is for the entire world now, not for Israel alone. Cornelius, a devout man but not a Jew, is one of the first non-Jews to be baptized. This universal offer of peace inspires awe and joy in Colossians and Ephesians. But, before we move to those letters, let's look more carefully at the significance of peace in Jesus' ministry as Luke presents it.

Luke's Gospel

Peace can be a word of greeting, farewell, or dismissal. Jesus, who has come to proclaim peace, does so when he sends forth the healed and forgiven (Luke 7:50; 8:48) who have received the blessing of peace and wholeness. Mark shares with Luke (8:48) the same story and the same ending: "Go in peace" (5:34, Mark's only use of peace). Luke, in parallel with Matthew, shows Jesus commanding his disciples to greet with a word of peace when they go out on their first mission (Matt. 10:13; Luke 10:5–6). It is peace that must be returned if the disciples are to stay and share the very presence of God through Jesus (Luke 10:16). Willful or hostile folk may be heedless of peace and miss it entirely, both in the present offering and again at God's final judgment. So "Peace be with you" and "Go in peace" are significant phrases, offering the blessing of God's presence for the making right of a life. Spoken at the end of an encounter, "Go in peace" acknowledges the blessing of God's presence, the creation of wholeness or *shalom*, and the promise that this *shalom* will abide.

All this said, we dare not miss Jesus' insistence that he did not come to bring peace but division (Luke 12:49–51), a sword in Matthew's version (Matt. 10:34–36; see also Luke 21:16). How did this one called to bring peace turn into such a harshly divisive savior? Most likely this statement reflects the real experiences of early believers. Divisions within families and among peoples, followed by persecutions, were part of the story of Christians, even as of the Jews, as they lived their faiths in a world not fully experiencing God's reign. We have seen that a true prophet tells the truth about real life and does not mislead God's people with false descriptions of peace. When Jesus speaks these sad—but so true—words of what will follow, he is proving himself a true and trustworthy prophet. Recall that Jerusalem itself and the great temple were destroyed in 70 CE, right before the Gospels were written. Then, as now, violence threatened God's creatures. Then, as now, God's creatures await a reign of peace.

Because of that long and bitter wait, perhaps we can better appreciate the jubilation of those in Jerusalem when Jesus finally arrived in the city (Luke 19:37–44; Matt. 21:1–9; Mark 11:1–10; John 12:12–18). Although the evangelists' stories are remarkably similar, only Luke's echoes the choirs of angels and speaks of peace. "Peace in heaven" the crowds cry out! *Shalom* permeates the universe all the way to heaven as the long-awaited king of peace comes to the holy city to take up his reign. As intense as the hope is, so also is the intensity of Jesus' grief in Luke 19:41. Jesus wept over the failure of Jerusalem to recognize "the things that make for peace," a failure that would lead to the destruction of the city. What did that jubilant bunch of citizens miss? Did they not understand Jesus' type of kingship? Or was it that they were not strong enough to follow up their joy with persevering faith at the time of Jesus' arrest and trial? If Jesus died to "keep the peace" as a form of crowd control by the Romans, what a terrible irony he foresees in this passage.

Yet the Gospel ends not with tragedy but with Jesus' greeting of peace (24:36). When he enters into the midst of his disciples, it is peace that he brings them. Now raised from the dead, Jesus is able to bring peace in a new and vital way. This is a peace that cannot be destroyed by death itself. It is peace from God who begins in raising Jesus to inaugurate a reign of peace. It is only as part of such a world of peace that the fullness of life and joy find a place. The beginning and ending of Luke's Gospel are marked by both peace and joy (24:52), appropriately connected to the disciples' "blessing God," that is, rendering thanks and praise.

John's Gospel

John's Gospel has little to say of peace until Jesus begins to speak to his disciples of his "return to the Father." In John 14:27 he promises them "peace." It is "my peace" that Jesus offers, not a peace identifiable according to ordinary human standards but peace from the One who alone can distribute what belongs to the Father. It is that great *shalom* that Jesus gives, a *shalom* that casts out fear and distress and should create joy. His speech ends with the same promise of peace, daring to offer it even as he faces crucifixion, because John's Jesus is certain that he has conquered the world, including death (16:33). As in Luke's Gospel, the resurrected Jesus greets his disciples with peace (20:19, 21, 26). Jesus breathes the Holy Spirit on the disciples after blessing them with peace and provides the power of God's presence so that they might live within the reign and power of God even in the midst of the world. That is the longed-for peace, given to them.

The Peaceable Kingdom: Jews and Gentiles Together

How would God bring even the Gentiles, not in covenant relationship of repentance and forgiveness, of faithfulness and worship, into a new age of peace? This is at least part of the question that beset early believers in Jesus. As the church spread beyond Israel and the Holy Spirit filled and inspired those who had "not known God" or been "far off," as the Bible puts it, that is, those of the "nations" and not Israel, how would they live together with their Scripture-loving Jewish sisters and brothers who sought to serve God according to their Bible? What would be the relationship of Jews and Gentiles who both believed that Jesus has been raised and was God's Messiah? For Paul this pressing question is engaged in particular in his letters to the Galatians and to the Romans, the letters in which he most often refers to peace. Paul is convinced that God is a God of peace rather than disorder (1 Cor. 14:33). On the basis of this conviction of God's ordered *shalom*, Paul makes decisions about human behavior in the young churches. Talk of peace becomes interesting as multiple voices claim that their ideas of order are the correct ones! This kind of argument has marked Christianity from its earliest days. Peace and justice must kiss each other; neither can by itself mark a Christian community. But justice in particular is a changing dynamic, as the voiceless begin to speak more and more. How do we make true peace? Who gets to decide what the proper order is?

Paul opens his letters with a prayer for grace and peace (Rom. 1:7; 1 Cor. 1:3; 2 Cor. 1:2; Gal. 1:3; Phil. 1:2; 1 Thess. 1:1; Phlm. 3), as do those who follow his style. No matter the apparent presence or absence of peace in the congregation to whom he writes, Paul's prayer is for the realization of that peace wrought by God through Jesus Christ. In Romans many references to peace follow that greeting. It is promised to all who do good, including non-Jews (Rom. 2:10). For Paul, the baptized have been blessed with

God's spirit and empowered to live as if God's reign of peace had begun. A sign of that reign is peace. He argues in Romans that both Jews and Greeks alike are caught up in the beginning of that reign of peace, thus making it possible to abide in God's great *shalom*. Romans 5:1, 8:6, and 14:17 remind his hearers that they have peace with God, for peace itself is descriptive of the domain of the Spirit. Paul calls upon the Romans to live that peace in an active process of peace seeking (14:19), and twice he blesses them with peace in God's name (15:13, 33). Perhaps this emphasis is a necessary reminder for fractious believers.

The great peace of God, now available through the Spirit's power to women and men, Jews and Gentiles, is precisely that *shalom* that marks God's presence, an ordered universe in which all creatures thrive and where justice does not create disorder nor peace get falsely created by injustice. Ephesians 2:14, 17–18 clearly states this animating conviction of early believers: "For he is our peace; in his flesh he has made both groups into one and has broken down the dividing wall, that is, the hostility between us. . . . So he came and proclaimed peace to you who were far off and peace to those who were near; for through him both of us have access in one Spirit to the Father." *Shalom* must include all God's creation: in Jesus it does.

Reflections

Every contemporary person, no matter how optimistic, is shaken by the widespread, intractable violence that covers our globe. Moreover, we have come to understand that violence done to the earth itself is destructive of God's *shalom*, that is, beautifully ordered creaturely relationships. In the New Testament, the Spirit empowers us to trust in, indeed to live, God's *shalom* even now. We can imagine God's *shalom*. We can trust God's promise that peace will prevail and even that peace has already gained the advantage in the resurrection of Jesus. Yet there is no doubt that our faith must fight against despair as we are called to pursue actively the blessed union of justice and peace.

Questions for Discussion

1. Some congregations include "sharing the peace" as part of worship. After reading this study, how would you describe what it means to share the peace? What implications does it have for life inside and outside the congregation?

2. Emily Dickinson wrote a poem describing the perfection of God's world as she viewed it one morning. It ends with the line, "God's in his heaven, all's right with the world." How is that statement similar to and different from what is understood in the Bible? Do you think it means the same thing as the cry in Luke 19:38, "Peace in heaven, and glory in the highest heaven"? Why or why not?

3. What do you think happens among us to create such a lack of peace in this world? Is there any way to begin to change our behavior?

4. How is peace different from lack of war? Brainstorm a constructive definition of peace. How might we pursue this vision?

Chapter Ten

Prayer

My house shall be called a house of prayer for all peoples.

Isa. 56:7

Prayer has been part of every culture everywhere in the world at all times and places. Human prayer, communication in some form with a divine being or beings, emerges almost naturally from a combination of forces internal and external to a human being. Think of the external powers so beyond human control: powers of creation and destruction, powers of renewal and erosion. Consider things ranging from wildfires to the conception of a child, from monsoons to malaria, from love to deep depression. All these mysterious powers have been and continue to be beyond human control (if not beyond human intervention!), yet they are matters of life and death. Life so often feels like our response to mystery and miracle.

Internal forces, as I use the term here, include the drive to respond to all those external forces, to one another, and even to experiences that seem most deeply hidden within us. Humans are irreducibly relational creatures. As we live, we find ourselves called to be grateful, to express fear, anger, and hope. To whom do we give voice to these internal sensibilities? Given the mysteries of our lives and our universe and given our nature as shaped by relationships, it is no surprise that people have over millennia drawn near to that Other who is mysterious yet as close as our breath. This is prayer.

The Bible as a whole can be thought of as a kind of prayer. It not only tells us of our forebears at prayer, but it draws us readers and hearers into communication with God. As we read stories and hear of all kinds of prayerful engagement with God, we ourselves are involved in communication with God. The Bible is all about communication with God and how such communication shapes human lives and, indeed, the universe itself. The Bible shows us a God who is irreducibly relational, who wants communication, creates the possibility of it, and initiates it over and over again.

From Adam and Eve to Revelation, song and speech to, in the presence of, and about God is a biblical theme. How else could it be? Here we are, trusting that a force we can experience in a variety of ways is also willing and able to engage us. Yet we cannot see God or Jesus, and the Holy Spirit is like the wind in these lines from Christina Rossetti's poem:

> Who has seen the wind?
> Neither you nor I
> But when the trees bow down their heads
> The wind is passing by.

So we pray to that power whom we cannot see yet whose effects we observe.

The variety of reasons to be in touch with God requires an extensive vocabulary of address, much but not all about speech. In considering prayer, we will look at words for "prayer" and "pray," but we will also consider "events" of praying. Why, where, when, in what circumstances, ways, and words do people in the Bible pray? What sorts of responses are given? Our examples will have to be limited, for the study of prayer as a biblical theme could stretch for a lifetime. The hope for this approach is that these examples may be paradigmatic, revealing some truths about biblical prayer that will serve ongoing immersion in biblical texts. In this section, our study will weave back and forth between the Old and New Testaments to catch glimpses of the prayer lives of the people of God.

The Story of Jesus' Birth in Luke 1–2

Luke's Gospel provides a description of the background of Jesus' birth and early childhood as a young Jewish child. Significantly, Luke begins by drawing back a curtain to show us the Jewish assembly at prayer (Luke 1:5–23). In the story of Zechariah, father of John the Baptist, we glimpse Israel at worship in accord with age-old traditions that include the ordering of the priesthood, the offering of incense, and the "whole assembly of the people . . . praying outside." It is in this context that Gabriel, the one who "stands in the presence of God," appears to Zechariah with a message unbelievably wonderful. The announcement of the impending conception and birth of John is an answer to prayer (1:13).

From this vignette, we learn that Jews prayed together and individually, regularly in worship and with reverence, and made use of incense, according to the commands of God. We learn that God hears, recalls, and responds to prayer. In addition, it is clear that the people are not surprised that God does this. When Zechariah emerges speechless from his encounter with God's messenger, the people understand that he "had seen a vision" (1:22).

In the rapturous encounter of Mary and Elizabeth (1:39–57), both women are caught up in prayer. Elizabeth speaks a word of blessing to Mary and her baby (1:42–45), while Mary bursts into a psalmlike prayer of joy, thanking God for the promised coming of Israel's savior. Mary's prayer of joy and thanksgiving repeats Scripture, particularly the Psalms. It is very like the style of Hannah's prayer in thanksgiving for a child (1 Sam. 2:1–10). Both these young Jewish women find prayer to be the right response to the gift of children they carry. Mary's prayer echoes the content and the pattern of Hannah's in a way that shows the continuity of prayer in the Old Testament and the New, from one generation to the next.

Three Points about Prayer from Hannah's Story (Judges 1–2)

Hannah's prayer resembles that of Elizabeth and Zechariah, who had eagerly desired a child even as they grew too old to expect one. They are part of a long biblical tradition of a child being conveived and born when by all human reckoning it was too late. Isaac was born to Abraham and Sarah late in their lives. Rachel waited long for children. Samson's mother, formerly barren, was told by an angel that she would bear a son. Her husband, Manoah, prayed that the couple might receive this gift of life properly. In these stories God's intervention was sought and received, and children were born. Such birth marks the children as special, but even more, it suggests that prayer for one's heart's desire is expected by God. This is the first point. "Cry out to me for what you want," God might be saying. "I am listening." Often, however, the lives of these prayed-for sons are not what the mothers had hoped. This is the second point. As we move through these stories, we should be alert to the ways in which God does and does not answer prayer.

One additional facet of Hannah's story deserves attention. Hannah is first shown praying at the temple of the Lord; there is no question that she as a woman may pray there. She makes a personal prayer in this public space. She is distressed, weeps, vows, and prays—all silently—and the priest thinks she is drunk from the gaieties of the harvest festival. (He is later persuaded that she is in earnest and offers his own prayer that she get what she wants [1 Sam. 1:17].) Similarly, at Pentecost (Acts 2:13), the disciples speaking and praying in the power of the Spirit are also deemed drunk by some who do not understand what is happening. The third point: prayer has a way of taking us outside ourselves, outside the norm, when we call upon an Other who is not visible.

Jewish Traditions of Prayer in Luke's Gospel

Luke grounds the story of Jesus in long traditions of a Jewish life of prayer and worship. Jesus is brought to the temple for purification, a regular ritual of Jewish life. It is there that he is identified as God's "salvation" by Simeon (Luke 2:30), an old man who regularly prays in the temple. Similarly, a widow, Anna, "never left the temple but worshiped there with fasting and prayer night and day" (2:37). Both of these venerable saints proclaim Jesus as God's own redemption, come to them at last. But our interest here is the life of prayer in which they as exemplary Jews participate. Jesus returns to the temple at age twelve, when the family makes a pilgrimage to Jerusalem for Passover, another time of prayer and worship.

Jesus prays at his baptism (3:21), at which point the Holy Spirit descends upon him. Catch the communication dynamic here. This Holy Spirit is God's response as well as God's power: communication is made visible as well as audible. Jesus prays at the time of his transfiguration (9:28–36), again in a way that results in visual and audible communication. In fact, Jesus' face is transformed as Moses' face was transformed when he was in direct communication with God for the sake of the people (Exod. 34:29–35, for example).

Lest we imagine that every prayer take place in a context of the revelation of glory, we need to recall two realities. First, Zechariah and Elizabeth had been praying for years, as had Hannah, Abraham, and Rachel before their prayers were answered. Therefore, we can say that perseverance in prayer, in communicating with God, is part of faithful human behavior and of discernment of our own desires and God's will. However, even a prayerful life can be disappointing. Second, God may finally not answer prayers at all if we pray, as we must, with limited awareness of the larger good and God's mysterious freedom. Jesus' prayer in Gethsemane, heartfelt and strong as it was, was not answered as he had most hoped: the cup was not taken from him. Job's original family was not returned. Jonah's desire to escape God's call did not succeed. And so it goes biblically.

Nonetheless, Jews were commanded by God to pray; prayer was at the heart of their lives together precisely because it was the place or situation in which their identity as God's people was most clearly acknowledged. Christians followed suit. We will look first at the commands of God that the people pray, then at the prayers they offer in the Old Testament, next at the Lord's Prayer, and finally at the way the early church began to pray in the name of Jesus.

Prayer as Communication between God and God's People in the Old Testament

People pray frequently and with great intensity in their encounters with God throughout the Old Testament. Consider Abraham and his ongoing interactions with God, which surely come under our "prayer as communication" rubric. In Exodus 8–9 prayer is the description of Moses' interaction with God, an interaction so palpably effective and ongoing that even Pharaoh commands Moses to pray (8:8, 11–12). Examples of prayer could be endlessly multiplied. Rather than look at every example, we will turn to two paradigmatic words about prayer. First, throughout Leviticus God sets up a system of communication through actions, aromas, and words in order that Israel might confidently address God. This is a system of prayer, where remorse, thanksgiving, hope, and belonging might be expressed both by an appropriate sacrifice of "pleasing odor to the LORD" (see, for example, Lev. 1:9, 13, 17; 2:2, 9). This is not our contemporary means of prayer, but it must be understood as God's provision of a means of communication for human beings who wished to express themselves to this mysterious and powerful Other without fear of being misunderstood. This system involved congregation and individuals.

Second, in Deuteronomy 6:4–9 (compare Deut. 11:18–21 and Num. 15:37–41) words central to the faith of Israel are given to God's people through Moses. First is a confession of who God is in relation to Israel, an affirmation of relationship and obligation. Then come the words describing a life of prayer. That confession of God and covenant was to be kept in one's heart (Deut. 6:6). It was also to be prayed constantly. Notice the words "recite" and "talk about" in verse 7. Notice also the commands "bind" and "write" (vv. 8–9). The prayerfulness of speaking to and about God, the bodily experience of God's presence in words, sung or worn, and the devotion of writing those words, a devotion later familiar to Christian monastics, are encapsulated here. In these two sections, each open to the infinite variation that humans create, public and private prayer is at the heart of being part of God's people. By no means do these two sections present the limits of God's call to prayer. In Deuteronomy 8:10, for instance, humankind is called to thank God for food at times of eating. Careful reading of Scripture will reveal God's call to be mindful in prayer of God's presence in each life and in the world. God's expectation is that prayer in public and private forms a people responsible to one another for godly behavior.

We have seen this life of prayer expressed by Hannah, Mary, Zechariah, Moses, Abraham, Esther, David, the prophets, Jesus, and countless others. In lament, in rue, in hope, in making a claim on relationships, in joy and gratitude and awe, people prayed with words, song, and dance. Prayer is not only about words from a book. The postures of prayer were numerous and expressive. We have come to imagine prayer as a mental activity, while our forebears knelt, prostrated themselves, stood, raised their arms, and generally engaged their whole bodies in these prayers. The life of prayer is so central to Israel's identity that Daniel risks his life in order to pray three times each day to God and God alone (Dan. 6:3–13). After having been saved by God from the famous lions' den, Daniel, as Zechariah centuries later, prays for the whole people (9:21–23) and is visited by Gabriel. His prayers too have been heard.

King Solomon offers our final glimpse into the prayers of the people of Israel (1 Kgs. 8:1–9:5). Solomon had assembled Israel for worship as the holy ark and vessels from the tabernacle were transferred into the temple. At this time of rededication to God, Solomon prayed aloud before the Lord and blessed the people that all the communication shared with God might also abide in their hearts. God responded, "I have heard your prayer and your plea, which you made before me." God promised that the temple Solomon built would be a trustworthy place for communication with God (9:3).

Life for Israel grew complicated in two ways. One is that which we have seen in Daniel, where Israel is in exile from the temple and scattered in distant lands. It is important to note how confidently Daniel prays to God even in a distant land, far from the temple. God was by no means confined to the temple. (This is also very clear in the books of Tobit and Judith.) Secondly, the hope of Israel, indeed, its confidence, is that God will be the God for all peoples. Isaiah expresses this clearly: "My house shall be called a house of prayer for all peoples" (Isa. 56:7). This hope and this tradition of communication with God move right into the New Testament.

The Lord's Prayer in Matthew and Luke

In Matthew and Luke, Jesus gives his disciples a prayer to pray with confidence that God will hear (Matt. 6:9–13; Luke 11:1–4). In this prayer Jesus summarizes the devotion to God and neighbor that marks his ministry. The prayer could have been prayed by any Jew of that time in terms of its content. Jesus' use of the word "father" indicated a strong bond with and a certain humbleness before God. He insists on this same humble posture for his followers, including those times he urges them to become like children (Matt. 18:1–5). Combine that sense of humility with the use of "us" language in the Lord's Prayer and this prayer acknowledges dependence on God and interdependence with one another.

This prayer of Jesus for his followers does not substitute for their regular worship in temple and synagogue. Jesus goes to synagogue "as was his custom" (Luke 4:16; 6:6; 13:10). He also participates in Passover and other major festivals in all the Gospels. (Such festivals, like Christmas and Easter for Christians, were times of prayer.) The disciples, while awaiting the coming of the Holy Spirit, the better to take up their task of witness, return to the temple (24:53) where they, like Simeon before them (2:25–35), "bless God"—that is, they pray. There they stay (Acts 1:14) until Jesus has ascended and the Holy Spirit falls upon them, significantly at the great Jewish festival of Pentecost, a time of prayerful thanksgiving.

The Early Church at Prayer: Acts 1–2

New and Old Testament stories, characters, axioms, and theologies flourish in a matrix of prayer. Prayer is as characteristic of those who follow Jesus as it was of those who came before them. As Acts describes it, the early church was constituted by praying together. Acts 2:41–47 describes how the earliest community remembered its own origins. Teaching, fellowship, eating, and prayers at home and in the temple mark the life of the community (2:42, 46, 47). As in the Old Testament, prayer was part of communal Jewish life in temple and home and was connected to meals. The first miracle of the early church happens as Peter and John are on their way to temple for prayer (Acts 3:1). The entire community later has an experience of salvation, albeit less than the full picture, in their prayer and care of one another (Acts 2:44–45; 4:23–31).

As the community spread out from Jerusalem, even when the disciples were separated from one another, they persisted in prayer. It is not incidental that Peter receives a vision from God as he is about his noon prayers on a rooftop in Joppa (Acts 10:9). Even more significant, perhaps, is that Cornelius, who was neither Jew nor Christian but devout, "prayed constantly to God" and was heard and responded to (10:1–4). His wonderful story begins to fulfill Isaiah's hope for God's house being a house of prayer for all people, even Roman centurions. For Christians, that "house" will not be the temple, but instead the new "body of Christ," the assembly of believers wherever they find themselves.

The Early Church at Prayer: In the Power of Jesus

In those priceless letters of the early church that make up so much of the New Testament, prayer is everywhere. Letters open and close with prayer (typical for all of the ancient world). Paul's consistently thanking God as he opens his letters (for example, in Rom. 1:8; 1 Cor. 1:4; Phil. 1:3) reminds us that all communication among church members was communication before God. For a Jew like Paul, "before God" means in prayer. Tucked away in 2 Corinthians 4:1–2, he provides a pithy statement of what it means to be an assembly of believers. It is by God's mercy that there is an assembly of people called together. It is in the sight of God that such ministry—communication of God's good news in word and deed—continues to be carried out. Paul describes the deep reality of life as God's people when he makes the claim in Romans 8:26 that the Spirit "helps us" in our weakness and "intercedes" at a level beneath our words when we do not know how to pray. Christians live by prayer, as did Jesus and his forebears.

For Paul the whole enterprise of communication with God has come to be possible through Christ's gift of the Holy Spirit. Paul often begins his letters with the invocation of grace and peace through God and the Lord Jesus Christ (1 Cor. 1:3, for example). In Paul's letters, prayer is carried out by those adopted as children through baptism into Christ who have received the Holy Spirit, which enables them to pray (Gal. 4:4–7). In some parts of the New Testament, prayer is explicitly carried out in Jesus' name, the new way of entering into relationship with God, the new grounds for confidence in being heard. We hear this message in Acts and in Hebrews with some intensity.

The presence or power of Christ does not always bring the desired answer to prayer. Paul's own story of not being answered as he had hoped is summarized in 2 Corinthians 12:7–10. Three times Paul appealed to lose the "thorn . . . in the flesh." Three times he was denied. Yet God's grace helps Paul understand that neither perfection nor freedom from the difficulties of being human are required to serve and communicate with God. Like Job, Paul is called to remain in prayer during the most dreadful losses and pain. A second story of an answer that is not quite an answer comes as Jesus sits at the Emmaus table the night after Easter (Luke 24:28–32). Cleopas and his companion are deeply sunk in disappointment that they have not seen Jesus, and it is already the third day as he had prophesied (24:21). But their later insistence that Jesus, though unrecognized, stay with them is its own kind of prayer. It is answered for but a moment, when their eyes are opened. Yet, immediately upon their recognition, Jesus "vanished from their sight" (24:31). Such a strange answer to their prayers for Israel and for themselves: it was a glimpse that allowed them and us to trust that Jesus may often be present and hidden at once. We do not get to abide in his presence in this world.

Reflections

Our inability to abide in the presence of Jesus is the same inability we have fully to know God's will and ways. We are brought face to face with our creaturely reality and the need for prayer. We are also brought to a new appreciation of God's will to be in touch with us. The people of God are not allowed to sulk, to go into their rooms and close the door. If something is wrong or right, we "talk" about it with God. Even if we are not "in the mood for talking," God calls us to shape our lives around the rhythms of prayer: Sabbath, pilgrimage, thanksgiving, the birth of children, even eating a meal. Lest we worry that we won't be understood, we have words and actions from God in the Old Testament and Jesus in the New, given to us to trust.

Questions for Discussion

1. In Acts 10, we see that even for Peter, the leader of this new group of believers, God's answer to prayer is often mysterious and indecipherable. How does Peter come to realize what God is seeking from him? What kinds of communication does God use?
2. How do you understand Paul's phrase "sighs too deep for words" from Romans 8:26? Have you ever found yourself praying in just this way, a wordless yearning for something or someone? What might such an experience teach us about the Holy Spirit's activity within and among us?
3. What is the most difficult thing about engaging in prayer for you? Do you see yourself or your community in any biblical stories?

Chapter Eleven

Reconciliation

All this is from God, who reconciled us to himself through
Christ, and has given us the ministry of reconciliation.

2 Cor. 5:18

Reconciliation is based on several fundamental assumptions
that point to the complexities of human qualities, expectations, and social arrangements. In order to reconcile, there must
be at least two individuals or groups who had a positive or neutral
relationship at one time. The relationship must have been broken
by some trespass or crime or insult. Both parties must identify
what would restore the relationship and then act to do so. To reconcile is to bring order to the disordered, wholeness to the broken, reengagement to the separated. It is a complicated process,
easily subject to misunderstanding, defensiveness, lack of honesty
about one's role, and all the other difficulties humans bring to
relationships with one another and God.

Yet reconciliation is also a priceless gift that enables life to be
lived more fully and deeply. In the Bible human beings are subject
to all the kinds of breakdown in relationships that we know from
our own lives. Even more, in the Bible the breakdown of relationships with God, as well as their restoration, is front and center.
How do we stay in relationship with a deity whom we do not see
but are called to love and obey? What happens when we do not?

How are we assured that our relationships with one another and with God have been made whole, given long memories and strong feelings? These are questions of reconciliation that the Bible explicitly puts before us in a number of places. Reconciliation is also an integral thread, questions about which shape much of the biblical dynamic from Genesis 3 to Revelation. In the ancient world, "reconciliation" was often part of the vocabulary of diplomacy, as "redemption" was of accounting. These words came to be used by creative theological writers to express aspects of the relationship between God and humankind.

Old Testament

In the Old Testament two distinct families of words have to do with reconciliation (itself a word derived from Latin). These words are translated in English Bibles by a variety of terms including "atonement," "forgiveness," and "mercy." These words have different nuances in English. We must start, therefore, with looking at how these concepts are interwoven. Basically, when the relationship between humans or between God and humans is ruptured, intentionally or inadvertently, God has provided in advance a way to heal the relationship so that satisfaction is made and the relational fabric of Israel's world is rewoven and strong.

For contemporary Westerners, it is not easy to distinguish the necessity of repairing relationship from managing emotional reactions. In order to understand these ancient texts, however, a helpful image is the reweaving of threads to make a strong fabric. God and humans belong to one another and function fully only as part of the one project of creation. In fact, "atonement" in its original meaning was "at-one-ment," bringing back into oneness. This sense of reconciliation will become visible in some New Testament passages, but it is an assumed aspect of every restoration after an infraction. Forgiveness, the willingness to forego justice in the face of sin, is a removal of sin and restoration of communion/ community. Forgiveness is a major step in reconciliation that also allows the community to be gathered anew.

It is God who forgives sins and God who reconciles. Exodus 32:14 can be translated, "The Lord is reconciled concerning the evil he said he would do to the people." The New Revised Standard Version translates this verb as "changed his mind," which is an adequate description of what God did. After Israel had not only created a golden calf but worshiped it and attributed to it God's own powers and mercies ("These are your gods, O Israel, who brought you up out of the land of Egypt" [Exod. 32]), God was ready to destroy them and start over with Moses alone. But after intense conversation with Moses, God was reconciled, presumably to the people, concerning the evil. God had changed his mind about destroying them all. God forbore taking all the angry action that had seemed fair at first. The fabric of the covenant relationship was to be rewoven, even though within that covenant God did seek justice for those who did not repent of their deeds.

God sometimes is and sometimes is not reconciled. In 2 Kings 24, Judah, the southern kingdom, has been beset by numerous enemies who have overwhelmed the kingdom and tried to destroy it. God does not prevent this overthrow of the people. The writer states his conviction that the people were being punished for the innocent blood shed by a previous king: "He filled Jerusalem with innocent blood, and the Lord was not willing to pardon" (2 Kgs. 24:4). The word translated "pardon" in this verse is the word for "reconcile" (in both Hebrew and Greek). God was not willing to be reconciled easily when Israel's people and its God-anointed king shed so much innocent blood that Jerusalem was filled. The blood itself cried out for justice, as Israelites had done so many years earlier under Pharaoh's brutal power. Brutal use of power has consequences for the powerful.

Solomon, well aware of God's freedom to reconcile with humankind or not, prays as he dedicates the new temple that it be a place where the people might pray and be heard, where reconciliation might take place. In 2 Chronicles 6:30, he prays, "May you hear from heaven, . . . forgive, and render to all whose heart you know, according to all their ways, for only you know the human heart." Again, the word "forgive" is a translation of the word meaning "be reconciled." Solomon pleads that the temple will be a place where God will look favorably on human yearning for reconciliation, a restoration of the community of God and people. It is clear that reconciliation is brought about by God, not by humans. It is, in a word, God's call.

Part of God's character, as we noted in the chapters on love and faith, is God's willingness to be reconciled even when the people are painfully lacking in love, faith, or even obedience. God is compassionate, the psalmist declares in Psalm 78:38. Even when "they" were not steadfast or true, God did not destroy them. When God remembered that they were "flesh," helpless to be as steadfast as God desired, God's compassion held sway. In their helplessness, God forgave, that is, was reconciled to, them. The relationship continued with humankind because God rewove it, since they could not. This sense of forgiveness and/or reconciliation is a precious word of how deeply the people mattered to God. God was willing to forego full investment in the covenant by weak humans just to be able to keep the connections strong.

On the part of the people, then, this mercy of God was the ground of prayer. In Psalm 79:9, all the singers plead to God, "Help us, . . . deliver us, and forgive our sins, for your name's sake." A profound prayer that calls upon God's power and character, it seeks the forgiveness (again, reconciliation) that relationship requires. Hope of being reconciled with God and enjoying the fruits of wholeness is expressed well in 2 Maccabees, an intertestamental Jewish work from the second century BCE. The book opens as a letter from the Jews in Jerusalem to their kin in Egypt. There is a prayerful introduction in which the senders of the letter pray that God will "hear your prayers and be reconciled to you, and . . . not forsake you in time of evil" (2 Macc. 1:5).

The Jews in Jerusalem were living through terrible times of extreme persecution. Martyrdom was the fate of many Jews who clung to God and refused to apostatize to please the Seleucid king. Again, the hope of reconciliation buoyed the steadfast. Hear the words of a brave Jewish youth: "For we are suffering because of our own sins. And if our living Lord is angry for a little while, to rebuke and discipline us, he will again be reconciled with his own servants" (2 Macc. 7:32–33). The grief, terror, and destruction being inflicted on the Jewish community had indeed torn the fabric of relationship with God. Where was God? Why did God not help? How could one serve a God so absent in times when the worst punishment was meted out to those most faithful? Yet hope for reparation, reconciliation carried out by God after a limited "justice" is served, allows this young man to address a great king with confidence and challenge. God's faithfulness and love encourage God's people to hope for wholeness.

Part of the encouragement for God's people to live in confidence of God's being reconciled with them as sinners—either purposeful or inadvertent—was based on the system of atonement that God had prescribed and promised to respect. In Exodus and Leviticus numerous means are provided for humans to make recompense for their sins. The means for restoring relationship vary according to deed and according to the economic situation of the one offering sacrifice. It is significant that the sacrifices and offerings are not on parity with the offenses. In God's wisdom, God has agreed to receive a designated token or sign from humankind as enough for reconciliation. Leviticus 4 and 14–16 provide particular instances of the means of atonement/reconciliation. Comprehending the system requires reading Leviticus as a whole. The day of atonement is described in Leviticus 23:27–32. This day is one in which a full Sabbath of rest from work or distraction is given back to God for reconciliation with God. This web of interaction between God and Israel could create great confidence in God's re-creation of relationships broken and jagged because of sin. God provided place, time, and means for reconciliation with the promise that such communication would be understood for what it was. That God commanded this symbolic system suggests that God ardently desired to be in a healed relationship and knew full well that humans on their own might avoid even the offer of mercy if it pointed out their shame and failure.

Exodus 25:17–22 offers us God's description of a place of reconciliation. "Mercy seat" in the New Revised Standard Version has a number of other translations. It is "atonement cover" in the New International Version, and "propiatory lid" in the New English Translations. It is a "propiatory" in the New American Bible and simply "ark-cover" in the translation of the Jewish Publication Society (1917). There is no single word to express simply what this construction is to be. God commands its form and explains its purpose. In Exodus 25:22 God declares, "There I will meet with you, and from above the mercy seat [which is positioned over the ark of the covenant] . . . I will deliver to you all my commands for the Israelites." This place of reconciliation sits atop God's law. God's meeting with Moses for the people's sake will be from a place of reconciliation, higher and weightier than the law. No wonder Israel is confident to pray that God will be reconciled to them.

At the end of Exodus, when all has been prepared in accordance with God's design and empowerment, God's presence is known in the tent of meeting, wherein is the ark of the covenant, covered over by this place of reconciliation. This mercy seat, or place of reconciliation, where God would meet Moses was holy because of the presence of God. Certain rules were made about who could draw near to it and how near anyone could come. Even the rules and warnings are merciful: God was aware that full visibility of God's glory would overwhelm the people and so protected them from it.

A full measure of the importance of the mercy seat can be glimpsed in Amos's vision (Amos 9:1). God's rage over the complacent injustice of Israel, its systemic sin, is so great that God proclaims from the mercy seat itself ("altar" is the NRSV translation) that the relationship is irreparably broken. There can be no reconciliation, no restoration of the bond between Lord and people. Yet the vision does not end there. Rather, God promises that not all of Israel will be destroyed (9:8–15). The vision itself is a terrible warning not to take for granted God's will to reconcile, for God will not be mocked by those who demand their own "rights" heedless of the relationship itself (see also Ezek. 7:11–25 and 43:18–27 for restoration of the mercy seat). At the same time,

God will not renege on God's promise to be the Lord of Israel. These verses gather up for us both the promise and pain for God of covenanting with humankind. This pain, the New Testament tells us, is fully expressed in the death of Jesus.

We dare not move on to the New Testament without some attention to reconciliation among humans. If reconciliation between God and humans is important in restoring the fabric of relationships from the village to the cosmos, reconciliation among humans is also vital. In Ezekiel 45:9–20, the prophet, in God's name, summons princes of Israel and people to just treatment of one another. Doing justice is a prerequisite to the restoration of the place of reconciliation; failure to do justice was a cause of its destruction. Here the "altar" is restored as the people restore their relationship with one another and God then reengages them. There is no separation between people's treatment of each other and their covenant with God. Humans can neither seek nor assume God's favorable disposition while ignoring each other's well-being. Reconciliation has to do with both God and neighbor. This also will be central in the New Testament.

Sirach, a wisdom-teaching book from the Apocrypha, is very interested in that interaction of God's mercy/reconciliation and that of humans. Alert to the dangers of arrogance concerning God, Sirach warns against human presumption of strength, power, and success in the world. Readers are reminded of the fragility of our human "strengths." Sirach 5:1–5 includes a pithy description of wrongheadedness, ending with the line, "Do not be so confident of forgiveness that you add sin to sin." This "forgiveness" is the word we have seen translated elsewhere as "reconciliation." Here is a warning not unlike Paul's in Romans 6:1, where he disallows even the question "Should we continue in sin in order that grace may abound?" as wrongheaded and dangerously foolish. One who is in relationship with God does not ask a question about what the bottom line amount of sin is: How much stress can this relationship take and still hold? This is the terrible human practice of testing God.

At the same time, Sirach—and Paul—know that God recognizes human limitations and for that reason reconciles God's self to humankind. The misery of death makes God patient and merciful: "The compassion of human beings is for their neighbors, but the compassion of the Lord is for every living thing" (Sir. 18:11–13). In this passage, God's reconciliation is the same as God's mercy; the two words are in parallel with one another. Sadly, the importance of reconciliation to human life is most clear when it has been breached. Sirach 22:22 mentions behaviors for which reconciliation is not possible among humans, including betrayal of confidences and arrogance. To destroy confidence destroys friendship (see also Acts 5:1–13). It is noteworthy in Sirach 27:16–21 that to be without the possibility of reconciliation is to be without hope for relationship.

New Testament

God's compassionate will to be reconciled with humankind is shown in its vulnerability and persistence in the story of Jesus of Nazareth. Nonetheless, the actual word "reconcile" is infrequent in the New Testament writings. The centrality and intensity of these few occurrences, however, outweigh their small number. We begin with Paul, our earliest witness to reconciliation in the New Testament. In two quite different letters to two quite different audiences, written in two quite different spirits, we find reconciliation described both in relation to God and humankind.

The Ministry of Reconciliation

In Paul's Second Letter to the Corinthians, he is defending himself against charges we do not fully understand *and* proclaiming again the greatness of the God he serves. Because of the fractured relationship between Paul and some of the Corinthians, he explores how Jesus' death and resurrection create a new way for humans to live together. Because Jesus died for all, all now may live anew for God. This newness, God's reweaving of the rent fabric of creation into wholeness, comes from God, whose will has always been to be reconciled. This is amnesty international indeed! God does not count old sins. This was proclaimed as God's way in the Old Testament. Paul is convinced that God has acted definitively in Jesus' resurrection to end separation between God and all people and creation. Jesus is the means given by God as the final sacrifice in the system described in Leviticus. As Israel was to have confidence in clear communication with God by means of sacrifices and pleasing odors, now Jesus' death is the last word in that system (note the "aroma of Christ" in 2 Cor. 2:15–16). Jesus' resurrection is the clear communication to humankind that God has been reconciled to those who believe in him. In a sense, God offers God's self in Jesus through the very system God had given to humankind, as the most profound communication of God's will to be reconciled. (No one ever said Paul's thinking was simple!)

The Levitical system helps make sense of Jesus' death and resurrection for Paul. New creation refers to the world in which reconciliation has happened at God's initiative for all people, not Israel only. The language of 2 Corinthians 5:18–20 includes references to God reconciling "us" and "the world" as well as reconciling himself. For Paul, this reconciliation is the very foundation of his own ministry. His call and challenge is to summon the whole world, whether Jewish or pagan in background, to be people of God. Reconciliation here is close to the idea of making peace between hostile parties. Paul never doubts human hostility to God, manifested in sin, anger, resistance, injustice, and the like. Paul's overwhelming joy is that God did not respond to that hostility in kind. Instead, God was merciful (or compassionate or forgiving: all words used to translate "reconcile"), reached out to humans, and did all that was necessary to restore the relationship. Such reconciliation ought also be part of the lives of the Christian assembly.

Paul speaks in Romans 5:10 of how humans as "enemies" of God were reconciled to God through Jesus' death (see also Acts 7:26 and 12:20 for a secular example of reconciliation of hostile parties). This reconciliation is the basis of the salvation available now through Jesus' life. The enormity of God's reach over the chasm that divided God from humankind is an important thread in Paul's writing (cf. Luke 16:26). The chasm has been bridged, the torn fabric rewoven; we "have received reconciliation." Paul comes back to this strong image in his complicated defense of God's faithfulness to all God's promises (Rom. 11:12–15). Assuming the "reconciliation of the world" (v. 15), Paul ponders aloud his deep belief that God will not abandon Jews who do not believe in Jesus. God's plan for "new creation," as Paul saw it, included the "stumbling" of the Jews in order to bring in the Gentiles (non-Jews). Riches beyond measure will follow the inclusion of Jews among God's saved ones, that is, in this new covenant. But their temporary "stumbling" is well worth it, Paul believes, if the reconciliation of all is brought about.

Both Colossians and Ephesians echo this message of the reconciling power of Jesus' death and resurrection. Colossians 1:19–22 speaks of Jesus as God's way of reconciling "all things" to God's self, including formerly estranged persons. Ephesians specifies the reconciliation of God's own called people, Israel, with the others who had not worshiped the one God with one another and with God: "He has abolished the law with its commandments and ordinances, that he might create in himself one new humanity in place of the two, thus making peace, and might reconcile both groups to God in one body" (Eph. 2:15–16). In Ephesians, this reconciliation is connected with the word "peace," picking up the sense of ending hostility.

Because we have looked at two different word families in the Old Testament, one often translated by "atone" in English, we should note that atonement does show up also in the New Testament. The similar ideas captured by the atone/reconcile duo can easily be seen in 1 John 4:9–10. In these verses God's love is the active agent, moving God to send Jesus into the world so that humankind could live "through him." This is, the writer says, the very definition of love: that God acted mercifully to renew the broken relationship with the world by sending the son as atonement for our sins. We are back to that Levitical system wherein God provides the means for clear communication of forgiveness.

This is a good place to take note that groups in the ancient world other than Jews also practiced sacrifice to restore divine-human relationships. Jewish roots are more pertinent to Christian development, but the ideas of sacrifice and at-one-ment would not have been alien to other ears.

Finally, the New Testament too picks up the concomitant need to be reconciled with one another. Matthew 5:23 makes the case clearly. You are called not to approach the altar with your gift to God knowing that someone is hostile to you. The need to be reconciled with one who is offended precedes coming to God with a clear conscience. The ancient prophets would understand, as perhaps do we. The more difficult reconciliation needs to happen first among us, who are each ministers of reconciliation as Paul himself was.

Questions for Discussion

1. To receive mercy implies that we face our own limitations and failures, the pain of which can be intense. Is pure mercy too hard for us to face or accept?
2. Have you ever been called upon to forgive and reconcile, or have you been the one forgiven or needing to be reconciled? How did you feel before being reconciled? How after? What helps us carry out these processes with one another? In larger groups?
3. In Sirach 27:16–21, to be without the possibility of reconciliation is to be without hope for relationship. Our contemporary world at the same time emphasizes and degrades human relationships. How might Sirach's wisdom help us reimagine relationships not only from a consuming point of view but as "pearls of great price"?

Chapter Twelve

Resurrection

Listen, I will tell you a mystery! We will not all die, but
we will all be changed.

1 Cor. 15:51

To understand the importance of resurrection in the New
Testament, where it is pivotal, we must understand its deep,
widespread, and varied Jewish roots. To find those roots we will
dig into a few places in the Old Testament. The "youngest" book
of the Old Testament is Daniel, written about two hundred years
before Jesus' birth. Jews by no means stopped thinking and writing about God and their world at that point. Considerable Jewish theological thinking from before and around the time of
Jesus is not included in the Old Testament. We will look at some
documents from the period between the two Testaments, the
time in which early Christian ideas and writings were being pro-
duced, in order to see additional development of thinking about
resurrection.

From Jewish and Christian writings, including the Bible, we
understand that there was disagreement about the idea of resurrection in the time of Jesus. Paul reportedly uses the open disagreement between the Pharisees and Sadducees to derail his own
trial (Acts 23:6–10). The Essenes may have had their own ideas as

well. Where did these ways of imagining resurrection come from, and what is the emphasis in each of them?

Old Testament

In Scripture, two theological affirmations are basic to thinking about life, death, and resurrection. The first is that God is creator of the universe, the source of all that is on earth, including the life of every creature. God gives the gift of breath to all that lives, and God has the power to stop giving such breath. God is, in a word, the Lord of life and death. Psalm 104 expresses this conviction in wonderful poetry. Addressed to God is the word of praise: "In wisdom you have made them all; the earth is full of your creatures" (Ps. 104:24). The power of the Lord to create and bring to nothing appears in verses 29–30: "When you take away their breath, they die and return to their dust. When you send forth your spirit, they are created; and you renew the face of the ground."

The second affirmation is that God is a God of justice. Justice is part of what characterizes God's realm. In the covenant with God's people, promises were made about their thriving, their reception of abundant life as they lived in covenant relationship with God. Even though Israel understood that both personal and national catastrophes might emanate from sin (departure from God's way), it was also true that the righteous/just and the unrighteous/unjust died. Sometimes evil was rewarded and goodness seemed to be punished. Spokespersons for God met untimely or violent ends. Life was clearly not just.

These two beliefs led to many questions, not least, When would God's promises of justice, of reward for the righteous, be kept? God's justness was especially significant for Israel, who believed that God had called upon Abraham, Isaac, Jacob, and their descendents to carry and manifest the truths about God to the entire world. How foolish they looked to the world, a people whose God could not or would not protect them and lead them into prosperity. The very faithfulness of God and Israel's self-identification as God's people was at stake for Israel when death seemed over and over again to destroy hope in God's promises.

Individuals and Life After Death
In several places within the Old Testament, we can glimpse the theme of resurrection. Although generally speaking, death came to all creatures, there are two or three who are reported as having gone straight to God's realm. Elijah was whirled up and away in a chariot of fire, never dying an earthly death (2 Kgs. 2:1–15). Enoch, a less familiar character, also ascended to God with no mention of death being made (Gen. 5:24). These are not resurrections, of course, because there is no death. But they are instances of human beings having some life outside of the earthly one. In fact, a few indirect references suggest that this form of life after earthly life was quite imaginable, if restricted to a few. See, for instance, Isaiah 53:8 ("taken away") and Psalms 49:15 and 73:24, where the psalmist expects to be ransomed "from the power of Sheol" and received by God. The stories of these persons taken by God without having actually died become a source of hope in the Wisdom of Solomon 4:11. In these verses, hope for life after death appears foolish to those who turn from God's way, but to the righteous it is part of their faith. The tradition of the ones who ascended to God becomes part of the hope for others at a much later date.

The Bible tells us of some who actually died and were restored to life by God's power. Two stories authenticate the claims of two of God's prophets to be speaking God's word. They also illustrate God's power over life and death, for no mortal could bring the dead to life on his or her own. Elijah restores to life the dead son of a grieving woman, who happens not to be an Israelite (1 Kgs. 17:17–24). The woman had trusted Elijah and his God in a time of brutal famine. In rage and grief over her "reward," the death of her only son, she challenges Elijah, "You have come . . . to cause the death of my son!" Elijah raises the boy to life and the woman responds, "Now I know that you are a man of God, and that the word of the LORD in your mouth is truth." Similarly, Elisha, also a prophet of God, raises a dead boy to life for his mother (2 Kgs. 4:27–37). Even the bones of the dead Elisha bring a dead man back to life (13:20–21). These are interesting and important stories, but by no means do they extend the idea of resurrection past the possibility of it for individuals.

There are also hopes for restoration to life for larger groups in the Old Testament. Certain promises point to God's refusal to let God's covenant people die out or disappear. Incidents refer to a return to life for Israel "dead" in exile, cut off from homeland, temple, and the promised land of God. God will not abandon the people in exile but will bring them back, restore them, raise them to new life. Hosea 6:1–3, a passage written during a time when Israel was besieged by the powerful Assyrian army, promises that "after two days he [God] will revive us; on the third day he will raise us up, that we may live before him." This kind of language echoes through centuries supporting Israel's hope. It will be applied to Jesus as the one God revives on the third day. In Hosea, however, it is the people who will be raised up.

The restoration of the people, Ezekiel's "dry bones" (Ezek. 37:1–14), offers similar hope. God declares to the prophet, "Mortal, these bones are the whole house of Israel" (v. 11). They know themselves to be cut off completely from God, dried up, dead. God raises them up and breathes upon them. (Echoes of this language permeate the Bible, from Genesis to stories of Jesus' resurrection and sharing of the Spirit.) The passage promises restoration of Israel from exile and the creation of a multitudinous nation (v. 10) in keeping with God's promise to Abraham. But it sets the stage for later thinking about resurrection, both because of the imagery used and because of the idea that God would not let God's people remain cut off. These scriptural passages were interpreted and reinterpreted over millennia in bodies of writing that range from the historical to the mystical. Personal resurrection of the dead is one interpretation that developed from Ezekiel's language.

Other Key Passages

Daniel. The prophet Daniel lived during an intense persecution by Antiochus Epiphanes in about 165 BCE. The book Daniel is filled with visions and predictions of what will happen when God acts on behalf of God's faithful. In Daniel 12:1–3 there is a promise. It begins with the formulaic biblical phrase, "at that time," the time when God will finally act. Change comes under the aegis of the archangel Michael. Daniel is told in a vision, "Your people shall be delivered, everyone who is found written in the book." (Jesus tells the disciples to rejoice that their names are written in heaven in Luke 10:20.) A resurrection is spoken of in verse 2: "Many of those who sleep in the dust of the earth shall awake, some to everlasting life, and some to shame and everlasting contempt."

In this resurrection, there will be a judgment of those who "awake" (not "all"). Indeed, this judging will be the work of the Son of Man when he comes at the end of days (Dan. 12:9–12). The summons in Daniel is to persevere in faithfulness to God, a strong word for a very difficult time when apostasy under torture was not uncommon. The loyalty of those who had died faithful to God might again make them look foolish and shameful. For them, the promised resurrection, with enemies consigned to misery and they themselves to heavenly existence, extended the timetable for God's faithfulness and justice beyond the grave.

Job. Job 14:12–14 has a number of interesting questions about resurrection based on the unlikelihood of it. Mortals die, Job says, and where are they? "Mortals lie down and do not rise again." Job wishes that he himself might escape the miseries of life in the finality of death, or, at least, death until "the heavens are no more" (v. 12). "If mortals die, will they live again?" (v. 14). If so, Job thinks, it would not be a bad bet to die and await God's call a second time. But he is far from evincing confidence in resurrection in this passage. "Will they live again?" There is no resounding yes implied to this question.

Isaiah. A much argued text also speaks of a resurrection-type event. Isaiah 26:14 simply declares, "The dead do not live; shades do not rise—because you have punished and destroyed them, and wiped out all memory of them." However, in verse 19 the prophet continues, "Your dead shall live, their corpses shall rise . . . , and the earth will give birth to those long dead." How literally should we read this? It is hard to say. In Luke's story of the father with two sons (15:11–32), the father unreservedly exclaims, "This brother of yours was dead and has come to life; he was lost and has been found." In this story the younger brother had not died biologically. He was described as dead to his family ("cut off" would be an apt phrase). When he returned to the family, Luke says he "came to life." Given the Lukan text, we must be cautious in reading death as biological and a return to life as the overcoming of biological death. In some cases that kind of resurrection—or revivification—is what happens (the stories of Elijah and Elisha). In other places (Ezekiel), new life seems to be more metaphorical. We might ask ourselves how we define death and whether it is different from the definitions of our forebears.

Intertestamental Works

After the death of Alexander the Great (about 330 BCE) and until the destruction of the temple and Jerusalem (in 70 CE) turmoil, strife, and change beset Israel. Many Jews lived away from their homeland. Those who remained endured regime changes, political commandeering of the priesthood, and attempts to hellenize Jews and Jewish life. People reacted in varied ways, from acquiescence to eager acceptance to rebellion and withdrawal. So distant was God's promised peace, justice, and abundance that theological creativity brought forth all sorts of fruits, including expanded thinking about resurrection.

The Maccabees
The four books of the Maccabees center on the persecution of Jews by northern kings. The story of the horrific martyrdom of

seven Jewish brothers, their grandfathers, and their mother is a memorable part of these books. The entire family dies willingly in order to uphold God's law and their traditions. While each of the books of the Maccabees takes a slightly different slant, all of them understand that there will be vindication for these faithful ones after death. Confidence in a resurrected life in God's presence enables the family to endure the tortures described. A key verse comes in 2 Maccabees 7:9: "The King of the universe will raise us up to an everlasting renewal of life, because we have died for his laws." When a brother offers hands and tongue to the torturers, he declares his hope that he will receive them back again from God (7:11). Yet another brother insists that he cherishes "the hope God gives of being raised again by him. But for you there will be no resurrection" (7:14). These martyred faithful, proclaiming God before the pagans, will be vindicated in accord with one reading of Isaiah 50:7–9. In 4 Maccabees, written slightly later and with a Greek philosophical bent, one hears more about immortality and eternal life as God's reward for obedience (see, for example, 4 Macc. 7:3; 13:17; 16:13). Bodily resurrection is not mentioned. With even these brief examples from the second century BCE, it is possible to see the variety of reasons and expectations for life after death. It can surely be said in general that God's faithfulness to God's faithful ones will not be stopped by death.

In a Jewish text from the time of Jesus that explicitly argues for an afterlife and against the belief that death is the end of the road, the claim is made that "the souls of the righteous are in the hand of God" and that it is only "in the eyes of the foolish [that] they seemed to have died." Their "departure" and their "going from us" was by no means the destruction it seemed in the eyes of unbelievers (Wis. 3:1–2). There is hope of life after death for the righteous even if they should die young. The wicked will have to reckon with their sins after death (4:20); at that time they will realize that they were the ones "who strayed from the way of truth" (5:6). "The righteous live for ever, and their reward is with the Lord" (5:15–16). God's justice demands this eventual outcome (5:17–20). A clear statement appears in the very introduction to this book, "God did not make death, and he does not delight in the death of the living. For he created all things that they might exist. . . . For righteousness is immortal" (1:13–15). As we pull these statements together, we find a lively witness to life after death as God's reward for the righteous, poetically summed up in Wisdom 5:15–16:

> But the righteous live for ever, and their reward is with the Lord; the Most High takes care of them. Therefore they will receive a glorious crown and a beautiful diadem from the hand of the Lord.

New Testament

Starting with Paul

Jesus' resurrection is key to the energy and confident hope of the New Testament, however that resurrection is understood. One strand of resurrection faith is that which we have seen in 2 Maccabees, the vindication of the righteous One who dies obedient and faithful to God, yet humiliated publicly. The martyr whose life and death witness to God is raised from the dead because God is faithful (see, for example, Rom. 1:3–4; 4:24; 8:11; Gal. 1:1; 1 Cor. 15:4; Phil. 2:9; 1 Thess. 4:14). For Paul, Jesus' resurrection is bedrock upon which was founded expectation of the future and wisdom for the present. Yet Jesus' resurrection alone could not create the communities, the confidence, and the new relationship to Scripture and tradition that we see in the New Testament.

A second strand of resurrection faith expresses the belief that all creation will experience resurrection through Jesus. The promise of eternal life is now opened to all the faithful righteous ones, including Gentiles. In raising Jesus, God showed power over death, the heretofore ultimate enemy of all relationships. Paul witnesses to resurrection hope in 1 Thessalonians 4:13–18. God will raise those who have died and those who are alive together at the second coming of Christ to "be with the Lord forever." Paul writes this to encourage folks who fear that to die before Christ returns will leave them out of the resurrection loop.

Paul struggles to write about what is unknowable ("in a mirror, dimly" in 1 Cor. 13:12) to folks equally struggling to comprehend resurrection (1 Cor. 15). Paul is convinced that Jesus' resurrection is a sign and the first fruits of God's ushering in a new age (cf. Gal. 1:1–3) for all who believe it. There has been a reversal of the death that came through Adam, for "all will be made alive in Christ" (1 Cor. 15:22), although it is not clear what this being alive will resemble. It will be glorious in a way appropriate to life in the realm of God the Spirit (15:42–49). "We will be changed," says Paul. There is no way fully to relate how we will be changed or into what forms, only that it will happen for those steadfast in the Lord (15:58).

For Paul, Jesus is the beginning of a new age wherein death does not have the last word. Persons baptized into Christ and living in accord with Christ will also experience resurrection either after death or when Jesus comes again. The Spirit animates the church and makes possible eternal life for all who walk by it. This eternal life is other than earthly, but it includes the eventual renewal of all creation (Rom. 8). The resurrection of the dead, the restoration of God's people promised in Ezekiel and Isaiah, is ready to begin.

The Gospel Writers

Matthew, Mark, and Luke all end their work with Jesus' resurrection. Either he appears as the risen One (Matthew and Luke) or the "young man, dressed in a white robe" promises that he is on the move again as the risen One (Mark). In his risen form, Jesus has great authority reminiscent of the exalted Son of Man (Dan. 7:14), and he commissions his followers, promising to be present or to send the powerful Spirit to be present with them. That Jesus is raised bodily is important to Matthew and Luke, who provide stories of the risen Jesus visiting his followers. Jesus still bears the wounds of his death, is able to eat, and spends time teaching. Bearing wounds and eating distinguish Jesus from angels; his resurrected body is the body of a resurrected human, not simply some heavenly being who never died.

Within these Gospels are depictions of eternal life that suggest that not everyone, not even everyone who calls upon the name of Jesus, will experience a joyful resurrection. Matthew's parable of the sheep and the goats (25:31–46) and Luke's of the rich man and Lazarus (16:19–31), as well as Matthew's parable of the weeds and the wheat (13:24–30) and Luke's story of believers seeking admittance to the great feast (13:22–30), tell us of eternal misery for evildoers. Paul likewise insists that evildoers will not "inherit the kingdom" (1 Cor. 6:9; Gal. 5:21), although it is not clear if they will rise to eternal punishment or simply abide in dusty death.

John's Gospel offers a different take on resurrection from the other Gospels. The primary distinction between John and other New Testament writers lies in John's sense that the reality of eternal life is in the "now." Jesus renames death. For him, death is glorification (13:31–34), exaltation (12:32; 3:14), a return to the Father. The believer in Jesus has eternal life (3:16, 36; 5:24; 6:47) and has already passed "from death to life" (5:24). At the same time, the claim is not made that these people will never die. So death is redefined in a way that has little to do with biology. Biological death is incidental, not because each person possesses an immortal soul. Rather, God gives the gift of life abundant and eternal to those who believe and obey the Son. John too shows the risen Jesus who can be touched but not held (20:17, 27), who eats, and who is strangely unrecognizable to those close to him (Mary Magdalene, his disciples [20:15; 21:4]). Jesus' resurrected body had moved into a different state of eternal life than he had previously occupied. So human expectations of eternal life, even for those who have it "now," must admit of postdeath transformation.

John's Jesus, like the risen Lord of Matthew and Luke, will be judge at the end time (6:39–40, 54). John 5:27–29 is a straightforward declaration that "the hour" has come when the Son of God–Son of Man will judge even the dead. The dead will emerge from their graves and live in eternal punishment or life. This judgment is God's judgment, which Jesus enacts (5:30). Here the Son of Man imagery is used fully. For those within the Gospel narrative and for later audiences, the connection between belief in Jesus and resurrected life after the judgment is unbreakable. Acts has a different word. Present experience is a "time of refreshing" "until the time of universal restoration" when the Messiah will return from heaven. Acts reminds its hearers that these times were long prophesied through Scripture (Acts 3:20–21).

Reflections

There is no single or clear resurrection thread to follow in the Bible. The Old Testament variably speaks of the resurrection of Israel as a people, the resurrection of the righteous, of martyrs who die witnessing to God, of all, and of no one at all. Life continues after death in the memories honored by one's family and through progeny. The Old Testament also witnesses to hope in God's justice, trust that God will keep covenant. Over time an expectation arose that God's faithfulness and righteousness not evidenced during people's lifetimes would surely be revealed in another realm, another dimension. This hope carried through centuries of turmoil and bore abundant and varied fruit in the century after Jesus' death and resurrection. For believers Jesus was the beginning, the pioneer, the first fruits of that great awaited day of the Lord. Jesus was the Son of Man who would come again to judge, and his resurrection heralded the healing of all God's creation at last. It also made possible broad human participation in that new age, albeit not yet full participation. (John's Gospel may be the exception to this.) The consistent witness is that followers of Jesus will find their lives caught up in the presence of God in a way that is joyful and satisfying beyond expression.

Questions for Discussion

1. How do we define death? Is it different from how our forebears understood it? The process of defining death is ongoing, probably never to be completed definitively. Why is it

important to define death? How does our definition shape our understanding of resurrection? How does it shape our lives?

2 Many writers and movie makers who specialize in horror, science fiction, or fantasy genres have shown us living—or at least moving—returnees from death. From zombies to ghosts to the restless dead, we fill our imaginations of what happens after life and what "surviving life" might look like. Why do you think human beings do this? What is at stake for us?

Chapter Thirteen

Word

The grass withers, the flower fades; but the word of our
God will stand forever.

Isa. 40:8

Jews and Christians, like their Muslim sisters and brothers, center their discernment of God in relation to God's creatures in
writings and contemporary words of promise. The importance of
"word" is a given. God communicates in many ways throughout
Scripture, but the use of words is central. As we consider this
theme, our focus will be on the word of God, leaving words
explicitly offered by humans and other creatures for another time.

"Word" as in "word of God" is a little slippery. First, although
we say "word" we really mean "words." "Word," then, is a kind of
shorthand for a spoken or written message. Second, when it
comes to "word of God," we have to decide how to understand
the "of" in that phrase. Does it mean word *from* God or word *about*
God? Third, Bible readers must always keep in mind that even the
words that are said to be from God are conveyed to us in human
speech through translations from several ancient languages. In
our exploration of "word" we will understand it as God's communication with us, both in messages from and about God that we
humans understand as words.

Finally, we need to remember that "word" is always part of a communicative process among people and between humans and God. Created and enfleshed, we people "hear" words not as abstract units of meaning but within the context of a relationship. Nicknames, including racial epithets, take on different meanings when spoken by different persons in different contexts. Tone of voice can turn "I love you" into a statement of devastating sarcasm rather than a heartening reassurance. Body language, to which we intuitively pay attention when possible, clues us in to the meaning of the words spoken. Words in a longer speech or an ongoing relationship have meaning not inherent in the isolated words themselves. Who has not lamented having their own words taken out of context?

Neither tone nor body language for the word of God are available to us eager interpreters. But we do have the long story, the relationship that helps make better sense of the word of God. As we move through the biblical texts, we will have to try to read God's body language and tone from the long relationship God has maintained with humankind. It is only a small stretch for us to think of Jesus as God's clearest body language, the word as human, the better for us to "hear" God's gracious word to us.

Old Testament

God Orders Creation by Word and Response

As suggested above, a word or message, even a word or message from God, is an event that involves at least two parties. God, as irreducibly relational as we know ourselves to be, utters a word that orders creation. Most scholars of Genesis agree that God, as Genesis tells the story, created all from nothing. God ordered chaos by speaking commands to all the stuff of the universe—light, water, planets and stars, vegetation, animals. God's word was heard and obeyed by all manner of creatures (see Ps. 104 for another excellent portrayal of such relationships). In Psalm 33:7, God is pictured as gathering "the waters of the sea as in a bottle" and putting "the deeps in storehouses." At the same time, the psalmist declares that it is by the "word of the Lord" that the heavens were made. Psalm 33:9 reads, "He spoke, and it came to be; he commanded, and it stood firm" (see also Ps. 148:5).

At the same time, the Bible also describes the creation as being the work of God's hands as well as God's command (Isa. 45:12 and 48:13). In these two interesting verses, God's word and God's action combine to create an ordered universe. Word and hands may be understood as describing God's intention or will and God's activity. We might also understand Genesis 1:2–3 in the same way. God's speech commands light even as God's breath or spirit (NRSV uses "wind") moves over the waters. In Ezekiel's "dry bones" passage (Ezek. 37:4–14), God also creates life from death. In that text God describes the process of bringing those bones to life, including "lay[ing] sinews" on the bones, causing "flesh" to come on the bones, "cover[ing the bones] with skin," and putting "breath" in the bones. These are very specific actions, none of which are described as creation by a word alone. The importance of activities in addition to speaking as God's way of creating and sustaining helps us see that the Bible summons us to understand God as personally involved in the world and seeking to shape creation as God wants it to be. Neither God's word nor God's hands that cover bones with skin are literally descriptive, but instead they convey to us the fullness of God's investment and desire for all of us creatures and the creation.

God's Word as Strong and Vulnerable

One way of understanding God's word, then, is as a personalized expression of God's will. Much as we believe that human beings express will and emotions through speech, so we describe God's expression of will and emotions as speech. We are amazed that God, creator, sustainer, and redeemer of this resistant creation, speaks to God's creatures. The desire of God to communicate with the living inhabitants of God's world is exemplified in Isaiah 65:1–2. Here God tells Israel that God "was ready to be sought out . . . , to be found," and that God indeed said, " 'Here I am, here I am,' to a nation that did not call on my name." It is significant

in this passage that God also "held out my hands all day long."
Here is an example of body language that clarifies the meaning of
"Here I am." It is possible that the words alone might be interpreted in a threatening way. The gesture of extending hands clarifies God's goodwill.

In this passage from Isaiah, God's own yearning to communicate has been falling on deaf ears. This tells us something additional about the word of God. Reponses to the word of God vary.
God's word can be resisted, as Isaiah suggests (65:1–6). God has
held out God's hands all day long "to a rebellious people, who
walk in a way that is not good" (65:2). God is very aware that
people may not hear (Ezek. 2:7). Indeed, Moses was challenged
right from the beginning not only by Pharaoh but by the very
people God had sent him to help (Exod. 5:21, for example). How
could he speak for God? Likewise, Zechariah, a prophet from
the sixth century BCE, speaks the word of God to people who
refuse to listen and who turn a stubborn shoulder (note the body
language here) and make their hearts adamant (Zech. 7:11–13).
People in other places in both the Old Testament and the New
doubt God's word and scoff at it (Judg. 6:13–17; 2 Chr. 36:16;
Mark 9:24).

God's word does not always gain its objective among those to
whom it is communicated. Eventually, we are told, God's word
will indeed have its way. But it is clear in the Bible that human
response is important to God and partly determines how God's
word lives among us. Human response is never the sole determin-
ing factor in God's desire to keep on communicating. God's promise to Noah (Gen. 6) and the resurrection of Jesus show us God's
response. Yet "word" is a two-party activity, and human response
is a vital factor in our relationship with God and each other. For
Christians, Jesus is a good reminder of two factors that are preva-
lent throughout Scripture. One is resistance to God's word by
humans, a resistance underlined by the crucifixion of Jesus. The
second factor is that God appeared to humans most often in
human form to speak a word. This second statement deserves
some attention.

How God "Speaks" God's Word

The most famous biblical example of God's self-revelation is the story of God's call to Moses from the burning bush (Exod. 3:2–6). This theophany (appearance of God) does not seem to come in human form, yet it is "the angel of the LORD" who appears to Moses (3:2). The voice does not emerge unmediated from the flames. Do these angels have human form? It seems that they are in glorious humanlike form, for they converse with humans (cf. Zechariah and Mary in Luke 1:11–20 and 26–38) and move about. Angels who speak as God (note Exod. 3:4) sometimes look exactly like humans. In Genesis 18:1–16, we are told that "the LORD appeared to Abraham." In fact, three men come to Abraham's tent at noontime. (The brilliance of light at noon highlights the clarity with which Abraham sees his visitors.) There is no hint within the story that either Abraham or Sarah recognize any of their visitors as the Lord. In fact, when one of the men announces that Isaac will be born, Sarah laughs. In this case only the readers know that the Lord is one of the three, a piece of knowledge that gives the story its engaging quality.

In a more obscure story, an angel of the Lord appears to Gideon beneath an oak tree and sits down there (Judg. 6:11–23). The angel comes to deliver a word from God, but this same angelic speaker is identified as the Lord (v. 14). Through the rest of the story the speaker is identified as an angel of the Lord or as the Lord, a fact Gideon does not realize until verse 22. The Lord has come in human form to deliver a message to Gideon.

In Isaiah 6:1, although God appears to Isaiah in full celestial glory, the more clearly to underline Isaiah's prophetic call, God is in humanlike form enough to wear a robe. Likewise in Jeremiah 1:1–19, when that prophet is called to speak the word of the Lord, God "put out his hand and touched my mouth"—a very humanlike move. God also appears to a variety of persons, including the prophets, to speak God's word. The word in these life-changing messages may be more powerful and persuasive when spoken by a human; it is also more vulnerable.

The delivery of God's word in human form is certainly not the only way it comes to us. God's word is delivered in many ways in the Old Testament, including through Scripture itself. Torah, Prophets, and Writings convey truth from God and about God to humans. As we move into the New Testament, we will see how important Scripture itself was for interpreting and evaluating the words and deeds of Jesus of Nazareth, in order to know if he truly was of God. Was he a true prophet, an authoritative teacher, or, as John's Gospel claims, the Word itself? To discern this was a vitally important process for Jews, who had been warned by God not to follow false prophets or to stray from God's word for them (Deut. 18:15–22). Also, all of God's creatures can bear God's message; even the winds become God's "messengers" and the fire and flame God's "ministers" (Ps. 104:4).

Yet the word comes so often in human form that the admonition in Hebrews 13:2 remains crucial for us: "Do not neglect to show hospitality to strangers, for by doing that some have entertained angels without knowing it." The admonition suggests that we might not be willing to entertain strangers or heed their message to us. This surely seems to be a human characteristic. Because the word of God the Creator should often come in human form lest it simply overwhelm the creature, that word is vulnerable to human inattention or rejection. How poignant is the vulnerability of Eden's creator, when the very first humans ignore the word in order to explore their own freedom. How poignant is the same grief when Jesus laments over Jerusalem's headlong rush away from the message he himself brings from God (Matt. 23:37; Luke 13:34).

New Testament

Two New Testament meanings of "word of God" are in direct continuity with the understandings of the Old Testament. One meaning is word of God as Scripture itself or as revealed in Scripture. A second meaning is word of God as the message preached *by* Jesus. Two new understandings, which gave rise to the New Testament itself, are the word of God as Jesus himself and the word of God as the message about Jesus. We will look at all four of these different takes on "word of God," observing both their interconnectedness and their areas of disjuncture.

Word of God as Message from God

The first use of "word of God" within the Gospel stories comes when Gabriel brings news of John the Baptist's conception to Zechariah in the temple (Luke 1:20). Zechariah, thunderstruck by the promise of a child in his old age, is not able fully to comprehend or believe what Gabriel says. "Because you did not believe my words, which will be fulfilled in their time . . . ," Gabriel says. The reader, like Zechariah, knows that Gabriel has spoken the words of God (see 1:19), which are a message to Israel that God has not forgotten them. The words are accompanied by both Gabriel's presence and the empowering presence of the Holy Spirit. When Simeon speaks his prophecy in Luke 2:29–32, when Zechariah sings at the circumcision of his son in 1:68–70, when Mary speaks her words of joy in 1:46–55, they speak the word of God in double measure: they are empowered by God's Holy Spirit, and they speak words from their Scripture, God's word treasured and written in past generations.

It is around the issue of the word spoken that people begin to wonder who Jesus is. In Luke 4:35–36, Jesus amazes a crowd by commanding a demon to come out of a local man. The people question each other, "What kind of utterance (word) is this?" Their consternation at Jesus' word is connected to its authority and power over spirits, not least unclean spirits. When Jesus wields God's commanding word in relationships with entities that other human beings cannot see, let alone command (demons, unclean spirits), Jesus is connected to God and not quite like his fellow humans.

People gather round him to "hear the word of God" and to experience healing, two closely connected activities of Jesus' ministry. They expect to hear the word of God, a message from God, from Jesus (see Luke 5:1 and 6:18–19, for example). People become convinced that "a great prophet has risen among us" because of the power of Jesus' speaking and doing God's word (7:16). Jesus identifies his ministry and that of his disciples as spreading the word of God. As he explains the parable of the sower and the seed (see Matt. 13:1–23; Mark 4:1–20; and Luke 8:11–21), the seed he has come to sow is "the word of God." It is a self-evident truth in this parable that the word sown will come to naught in some cases but that it also will amaze by its prolific fruitfulness in others. Part of the point of that parable is that the sower cannot control where the word will bear fruit.

This word of God that Jesus brings needs to be heeded or obeyed, a point that emerges from the parable of the sower. It also shows up in statements from Jesus such as "Blessed rather are those who hear the word of God and obey it" (Luke 11:28) or the parables of the person who built his house on rock instead of sand (Matt. 7:24–27; Luke 6:47–49). Hear Jesus' words, the word of God, require a human response or the consequences will be the destruction of life. Jesus is speaking God's truth about how things are, how things work, and about the shape and direction of God's creation. These words are not to be thought trivial. Jesus insists (Matt. 24:35; Luke 16:17) that his "words will not pass away" even if the creation (heaven and earth) does. These are the words of God. They are true into God's future, which is not limited by the existence of the present cosmos.

Word of God as Scripture

Those who believed in Jesus generally accepted earlier Scripture as the word of God and true forever. Acts 4:23–32 portrays these convictions in a story. Jesus' disciples have gathered after the release of Peter and John from prison. In the course of their celebration, they pray together to God the Creator who had "said by the Holy Spirit through our ancestor David . . ." They then quote two verses from Psalm 2. In this account Scripture is clearly God's word. Furthermore, Scripture is quoted because the disciples find it immediately applicable in their own situation (see Acts 4:27–28). Because of their confidence that God's scriptural word continues to be true when properly interpreted, they also pray to speak God's word "with all boldness" (v. 29), a petition granted (v. 31. In this understanding, the word of God remains continuous and moves into the future. Scripture does require interpretation, however. The risen Jesus teaches the disciples how to understand Scripture in Luke 24:27. The disciples speak with the same authority as that which David had—that of God and God's spirit.

Paul speaks of Scripture almost as a person who bears the word of God in a trustworthy way. This is most clear in Galatians 3:15–16, where Paul argues for Jesus as the offspring of Abraham to whom God's promises were made. Paul's argument turns on the fact that the word "seed" in Scripture (Gen.12:7) is singular, not plural. For Paul then it is clear that God's promising word is accurately conveyed in Scripture through the details of the grammar itself. Also in this same chapter, Paul refers to Scripture as "imprison[ing] all things under the power of sin" (3:22) and the law (torah) as a "pedagogue." He does not use the phrase "word of God," but he certainly shows us how this scriptural word of God continued to exist and matter.

Jesus as Word of God

How does an invisible God communicate with humankind? For centuries Jews had understood the word or message (*logos* in Greek), whether written or spoken, as God's will mediated to humans. Jewish tradition took the mediator to be in some way fully God (though not the whole of God). Wisdom was certainly one such mediator, personified as a woman in Proverbs 8, for example. The word of God might also be symbolized as a warrior: "Your all-powerful word leaped from heaven, from the royal throne, into the midst of the land that was doomed, a stern warrior carrying the sharp sword of your authentic command, and stood and filled all things with death, and touched heaven while standing on the earth" (Wis. 18:15–16). Both as woman and warrior, servants of God, the word "conquered the wrath not by strength of body, not by force of arms, but . . . appealing to the oaths and covenants given to our ancestors" (Wis. 18:22). Philo, a Jewish theologian, spoke of the *logos* (word) as mediator of God.

John's Gospel teaches that God's *logos* took on the human form of Jesus of Nazareth (John 1:14). Not only does Jesus speak God's word and wield divinely given power to effect God's will (as do other humans in Acts in the power of the Holy Spirit), but Jesus is that mediator, that word. God's word has flesh and is God's presence among humans. John's Gospel understands this as Jesus' particular reality, unlike the prophets or any others before Jesus (John 1:18).

Word of God as the Word about Jesus

It is a small step from Jesus as God's word to understanding the message about Jesus as God's word. The writer of Ephesians asks for prayer to enable him to speak a message, "the mystery of the gospel," with boldness (Eph. 6:19; see also 1:13, where the "word of truth" is the "gospel"). Likewise in Colossians 1:25–27, the writer understands himself as given a commission to "make the word of God fully known." That word is about Christ (see also Col. 4:3).

Reflections

A connection between the word of God in the Old Testament and through Jesus is made directly in 1 Peter 1:23–25. The writer tells believers that they "have been born anew, not of perishable but of imperishable seed, through the living and enduring word of God." He then quotes Isaiah 40:6–9, an ancient passage on the brevity of human life and the enduring nature of God's communication with humans ("the word of the Lord endures forever"). In verse 25 he claims that Jesus is the chief bearer of God's word, indeed God's communicative word itself. "That word," writes Peter, "is the good news that was announced to you."

Questions for Discussion

1. What are some of the ways we might learn of God and God's will? Which ways do you most trust?

2. Do you see any dangers in the conviction that one has received a "word from God"? How does a community establish the truth or value of such claims?

3. Do you think that there are experiences that are beyond words? How do we tell one another about such experiences? What "language" do we use?

4. Do you believe that verbal communication tells truth more fully than nonverbal communication? Can you give some examples from your own experience?